This isn't just a mental health buzzword; it's a lived experience that brings the overcomer spirit to your very own story. We all have a mind, body, and spirit. Dayne knows the depths of what breaking free from the torment that can plague us as mere humans looks like. He's traversed the dark places and discovered the glorious light that sustains us and ultimately helps us flourish. *Choose Prayer, Not Despair* has a vital key to your well-being. Unlike the hidden agendas of some popularized solutions, this one has eternal staying power, and Dayne has the story, heart, humility, and headspace to help you live a life in full freedom and authority, because he points to the One who is our ultimate helper.

—Tamra Andress
Global Podcaster, Speaker, and Movement
Maker

Choose Prayer, Not Despair is a beacon of hope for anyone walking through the shadows of mental health struggles or standing beside someone who is. Dayne's words radiate compassion, authenticity, and unwavering faith, reminding us that no valley is too deep for God's light to reach. This book is a lifeline for those who have been seeking a solution to get through life's most challenging struggles.

Dayne seamlessly blends personal testimony with the transformative power of Scripture, creating a guide that speaks directly to the heart. The prayers woven throughout are not mere words but invitations to encounter the healing presence of God in the midst of pain. If you're searching for peace, longing for freedom, or simply needing to be reminded that you are not alone, *Choose Prayer, Not Despair* will meet you right where you are.

Dayne's vulnerability and trust in God's promises will inspire you to believe again—for yourself or for someone you love. This book is a gift of hope, a call to deeper faith, and a testament to the relentless love of a God who never lets go. I wholeheartedly recommend *Choose Prayer, Not Despair* to anyone seeking comfort, restoration, and the courage to press on.

—JOSIAH ALIPATE
YOUTH PASTOR, DIGITAL EVANGELIST, SOCIAL
MEDIA INFLUENCER

CHOOSE
PRAYER
NOT DESPAIR

CHOOSE
PRAYER
NOT DESPAIR

DAYNE KAMELA

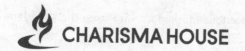

CHARISMA HOUSE

While the author has made every effort to provide accurate, up-to-date source information at the time of publication, statistics and other data are constantly updated. Neither the publisher nor the author assumes any responsibility for errors or for changes that occur after publication. Further, the publisher and author do not have any control over and do not assume any responsibility for third-party websites or their content.

For more resources like this, visit MyCharismaShop.com and the author's website at LitWithPrayer.com.

Cataloging-in-Publication Data is on file with the Library of Congress.

International Standard Book Number: 978-1-63641-462-1
E-book ISBN: 978-1-63641-463-8

1 2025
Printed in the United States of America

Most Charisma Media products are available at special quantity discounts for bulk purchase for sales promotions, premiums, fund-raising, and educational needs. For details, call us at (407) 333-0600 or visit our website at charismamedia. com.

This book is dedicated to my mother, Sierra Kamela, whose unshakable faith in God, unwavering love, and belief in my healing helped me most during my mental health crisis. I love you so much, and your influence on my life and faith has greatly shaped my life's calling. Thank you for standing by my side over the past five years as I've shared my faith online, always being there to encourage, support, and pray for and with me. May the Lord continue to use your incredible gifts to be a light in this world and a blessing to everyone you encounter.

CONTENTS

Foreword

As a pastor, I am privileged to witness incredible transformative moments in people's lives. However, this particular journey is very personal to me. I saw firsthand what my cousin Dayne experienced. I had a front-row seat to his struggles, his questions, and ultimately his incredible transformation. Watching his story unfold was not just inspiring; it was a testament to the power of God's grace and life-changing impact.

Choose Prayer, Not Despair invites anyone struggling with fear, mental health issues, or spiritual uncertainty to embrace a life of deeper faith and discover the hope only God can provide.

In these pages, Dayne shares an honest account of his struggles and the valuable lessons he learned. More importantly, he offers practical tools and biblical truths to help others experience the same transformation. Prayer sustained him through difficult challenges and became the foundation for his healing and renewal. I believe that what God did in his life, He can do for anyone. This book serves as a guide—a road map for navigating life's darkest valleys and finding the light of God's presence even in the midst of a storm.

As you read, open your heart to the possibility of change. Allow the prayers, testimonies, and biblical insights to draw you closer to the God who listens, loves, and heals. I pray you will experience the overwhelming peace and abundant life that come from a deep relationship with Christ.

This isn't just a book about prayer—it's a lifeline, an invitation to trust God wholeheartedly, and a reminder that despair doesn't have to define your story.

—Aryan Wallwork
Lead Pastor, His Church AZ

Introduction

I WAS RUNNING DOWN the freeway, my brother's Bible clenched tightly in my hand, my heart pounding as hard as my feet hitting the asphalt. Cars raced by, horns blaring, drivers staring—but I couldn't stop. I was headed from Phoenix to Los Angeles on foot, as if nothing could stand in my way. This wasn't just a sprint; it was the beginning of a descent into the chaos of mania, a journey that would reveal more about my mind, my faith, and my deepest battle against the darkness of the unseen realm.

As a child, I was more fearful than my older brother and sister. When they were each four years old, they took two weeks of private swimming lessons and learned to swim on their own. When I turned four, my mother took me to the same swim instructor. Over the two-week course, I only managed to put my face in the water. I was so afraid that it took me two weeks to complete the first step in becoming a swimmer. I eventually learned to swim with more lessons, but due to my anxieties, it took me much longer than my siblings. My younger brother, at four years old, learned to swim before I did.

Growing up, I continued to be a more worrisome and fearful kid, at least in comparison to my three siblings. The only other person who worried a lot in my family was my maternal grandmother. My grandparents lived close by, so my grandmother often babysat and took care of us. She was a prayer warrior and a lifelong worrier. She prayed hard for all of us as we grew up, hoping that one of her grandchildren would serve in ministry. She thought it would be my younger brother, but God had other plans.

When I was in my early teens, my grandmother suffered a major mental health crisis from which she never recovered. She soon went on to be with the Lord, leaving our family—and my mother in particular—with many questions. We all prayed and believed for a healing that never came in this life.

I would also struggle with my own health, my mental health. Satan came to try to steal, kill, and destroy my mind, my gifts, and my future. But I know Jesus came so that I might have life and have it more abundantly (John 10:10). God turned the enemy's plan around for my good (Gen. 50:20) and gave me a platform to declare His grace and glory through the power of prayer.

The subject of mental health covers a wide spectrum of ailments, beginning with anxiety, worry, and fear, then extending to deep depression and more severe conditions that can require lifelong medication, intense therapy, and ongoing struggles. I need to tell you up front that I wholeheartedly believe in God's power to heal and the effectiveness of healing prayer. At the same time, I know therapy and medication can have positive, even life-changing, effects. So if you're struggling with your mental health, I know this book will be helpful to you, but please consult a doctor or therapist as well. Each person's health journey is unique and follows its own path.

As for me, I suffered a major mental breakdown and was diagnosed with bipolar disorder in my early twenties. By God's grace, I was supernaturally healed. In the following chapters I will discuss mental health primarily from a spiritual perspective, exploring how God healed me through the power of prayer in Jesus' name and how men and women in the Bible dealt with depression and despair. Scripture tells us how Jesus healed many people with mental health disorders, though they were identified differently then.

We will also discuss the rise in mental health issues today and the role demonic forces play. I believe people can open doors to spiritual attack, but I also believe my story and the lessons I learned will help you close those doors and recognize the danger signs.

This book offers hope and encouragement for anyone dealing with mental health issues or supporting a loved one who is struggling. Praying God's Word over your mental health can bring both physical and emotional healing. God is not a respecter of persons (Acts 10:34, KJV), and what He has done for me, He can do for you.

In the pages ahead you'll journey with me through some of life's darkest valleys and witness how God's light broke through—even when all hope seemed lost. You'll see that His love is relentless, pursuing us in the midst of fear, despair, and even our most chaotic moments. Whether you're grappling with pain or running from it, God's presence is never far away.

To support you on this journey, I've included prayers you can use for yourself or a loved one. These prayers aren't magical formulas; their power lies in being rooted in the living Word of God (Heb. 4:12). They are simple yet profound tools for connecting with the One who brings true healing and restoration.

My prayer is that this book will strengthen your faith and give you the confidence to believe that God is both able and willing to heal your mental health, allowing you to step into the abundant life He desires for you—a life of freedom and wholeness. He knows your pain and has already made a way for your healing. If you're willing to take the first step toward Him, you'll discover a hope greater than any fear, a peace that withstands the fiercest storms, and a purpose that transforms even the deepest pain. God's love has the power to turn your darkest struggles into a radiant testimony of His grace. Let's take this journey together.

PART I

WHY PRAYER?

Chapter 1

HOW PRAYER SAVED ME FROM AN INCURABLE MENTAL ILLNESS

I STARTED FOLLOWING JESUS when I was eighteen years old. Although I was raised in the church and considered myself saved, I didn't really know Jesus or practice my faith besides going to church. Looking back now, I wish I had encountered Jesus sooner, but God used my mom to plant those seeds of faith within me and my siblings as we were growing up.

Within a six-year window, my parents had four kids: my sister, Danielle; my older brother, Ross; me; and my younger brother, Sean. When we were young kids, my mom and grandparents would take us to church and Sunday school. During summer breaks when the dates worked out, she would send us to church camp, which she hoped would impact our faith.

My mom asked God to do His work in us in His unique way and did not force religious rules down our throats. She would be the first to tell you she never imagined one of her kids would end up in full-time ministry. I've heard numerous stories of young adults walking away from their faith because of how their Christian parents made them feel. It's sad to see, but I empathize with those young adults. I don't know where I would be now if my mom had done the same with me and my siblings. Fortunately, many of these young people are being reached with the love of Jesus through digital media. God is moving and bringing His children back.

The Encounter

I decided to start following Jesus in my first year of community college. My mom wanted to visit a new church that was expanding into Scottsdale. I went along because I still lived in Arizona and attended church with my mom as often as I could.

When we arrived that Sunday, I got ready to do what I always did: zone out until it was time to leave. This day was different. You may be thinking the message must have been some deep prophetic word that pierced my heart, but it was the complete opposite.

The sermon was titled "Think Like a Billionaire," a topic that piqued my interest right away. Being in my first year of college, I wanted to learn how to become financially successful, so the pastor had my attention. As it turned out, the message wasn't really about making money. It was about how the secular world views success. Funny yet practical, the message did a great job of helping us understand that the billionaires mentioned in the sermon were successful because their worldviews were influenced by biblical truths.

I was so inspired by the sermon that I rededicated my life to Christ and decided to start getting to know Jesus. My commitment was genuine, and it showed. My mom could see that her son had changed—that I had found a new direction and a renewed purpose for my life.

The Call

The Bible tells us that God has uniquely gifted each of us to serve His kingdom purpose on earth. He has given us gifts and callings that are irrevocable (Rom. 11:29), meaning He will not take them back. These gifts can involve serving, encouraging, leading, and teaching, among others. They are meant to be shared, enriching the lives of those around you and bringing glory to God.

As we grow in our relationship with God, we begin to uncover the unique gifts He has placed within us and learn how to use them effectively in different areas of life. This might mean leading a family with love and wisdom as an amazing mom or dad, or leading in other spheres—whether in business, ministry, the nonprofit sector, politics, sports, entertainment, or beyond. Whatever arena you're called to is important to God. By sharing your gifts with others, you are fulfilling God's purpose for your life and becoming a vessel of His love, impacting the world.

Jesus taught us that the greatest commandment is to love the Lord your God with all your heart, mind, soul, and strength, and the second is to love your neighbor as yourself (Matt. 22:37, 39). Many people overcomplicate finding their purpose, but it really comes down to these two things: loving God and loving others. We love God by living in a way that pleases Him and by using the gifts He's given us to serve those around us. Through prayer we connect with God, seek His guidance, and develop our gifts to fulfill His will.

Deciding to follow Jesus changed me completely. I felt a renewed excitement for life and for the ways God could use me to serve others. Looking back, I realize God was beginning to awaken gifts within me that had been lying dormant. I'd always wondered why I was such a shy, fearful kid, but I discovered that much of it came from not knowing who I truly was in Christ. As I embraced my identity in Him, a new spirit of hope, joy, and confidence began to emerge. When you pursue knowing God, He reveals who you truly are—uniquely created, highly favored, and unconditionally loved (Jer. 29:13).

As my relationship with God grew, so did a desire to encourage myself and others. This became a driving force in my life, even before I fully understood it. God was showing me one of the gifts He had placed in me. When you come to know the Lord, He reveals not only who you are but also how He's designed you to impact His kingdom. First, you discover your gift; then you develop it; and finally, you deploy it.

When I discovered this gift of encouragement, all I wanted was to use it. Whether it was praying on my way to school to encourage myself or encouraging my friends, family, and coworkers, I found a purpose beyond myself. Each day my mission became to know God more deeply and to serve others through my gift of encouragement.

THE ATTACK

It had been four years since I decided to follow Jesus, and I was now in my last year of college at Arizona State University. I was earning a bachelor's degree in exercise and wellness, which was a passion of mine. I had a great job at a sports performance facility, where I was training young athletes, and I had my own personal training business on the side. Spiritually and professionally, my future looked bright.

At the time, I was living at home to save money and to help support my parents, who were going through financial difficulties following the 2008 real estate crash. My younger brother, Sean, was also back at home after leaving the Naval Academy. He'd been recruited to play football but had sustained injuries that kept him from participating, so he decided to leave the academy and received an honorable discharge. As a trainer, I worked with him to lose over fifty pounds and get into the best shape of his life, even with his back injury.

Sean was still figuring out what he wanted to do with

his life, and I did my best to encourage him to explore his God-given gifts. I was the one in the family who was always excited about what God was doing, and I loved sharing this with everyone. Our family is very close and enjoys spending time together, which made living under the same roof a truly rewarding experience.

During these four years, I became deeply invested in reading anything that could help me develop the skills I needed to fulfill my calling. I formed the habit of reading one or two professional development books each week, becoming increasingly obsessed with self-help and personal growth. I believed that improving myself would enable me to help others around me do the same. My ability to process and apply new information quickly allowed me to learn efficiently, leading to rapid progress.

Though this was a blessing, it also had a dark side. As I grew intellectually, I found myself reading less of the Bible. I mistakenly believed the knowledge I gained from other books could be more helpful to me. My prayer life remained strong, but neglecting Bible study left me spiritually unprepared for the challenges I would face. I didn't fully understand God's Word or how to use it to protect myself from the enemy's attacks.

My growing obsession with personal development began to impact my behavior, especially around my family. I became more intense in my pursuit of growth, almost pushing my family to follow suit. My speech became faster, and I grew more hyper and enthusiastic about everything I was learning. Satan saw an opportunity to twist my strengths, and my gift for quick learning began to work against me.

As I became more consumed, I started to sense a dark presence in my life that I didn't quite understand. Because I was ignorant of the Word, I entertained this presence rather than rebuking it. The enemy began to oppress my mind. At first the thoughts didn't seem dangerous—just strange. I believed I was part of a greater plan, chosen for something unique. I thought I needed to go to Hollywood and pursue acting, or go to clubs to spread the gospel and get people so excited about Jesus that they didn't want to drink. I accepted these bizarre ideas without seeking God's guidance, continuing to spiral for months until I found myself in a full-blown manic episode that would compel me to take my sister's car one morning and drive to California.

I didn't pack anything, but I took my brother Sean's Bible. My journey took a brief detour when I clipped the back of my sister's car at seventy miles per hour while merging onto the highway. Barely regaining control of the car, I snapped back to reality. Realizing the danger I was in, I pulled over to the side of the freeway. After catching my breath, I decided to run to California. I got out of the car with my brother's Bible in my hand, watching cars rush by for a few moments, and then proceeded to run along the side of the freeway. After maybe fifty yards I started walking until I heard the sound of police sirens behind me and loud voices saying, "Get down on the ground!" I complied and was handcuffed and put in an ambulance, where the paramedics tested my blood to see what I was on. Nothing registered on the tests, so I was taken to the hospital because they all knew something was wrong.

My family arrived at the hospital, and still being in a delusional state, I agreed to admit myself to a behavioral health hospital. I believed everything happening was part of a grand plan, not fully understanding the seriousness of my situation. I spent two weeks in this hospital, where the doctors gave me various medications to calm me down. The psychiatrist assured my mom that these strong cocktails would bring me back to reality. But during that time, I experienced overwhelming darkness, fear, and oppression. It was the hardest period of my life. Words can barely describe the despair I felt.

I felt like God had abandoned me and all the good things in my life were now gone. It was the darkest time I had ever known, and I felt utterly helpless. After being released from the hospital with prescriptions for several medications, I sought help from a Christian psychologist who specialized in ADHD/ADD and used brain mapping and biofeedback to assess my brain function. The brain map revealed that I had severe bipolar 1 disorder and ADHD. I was told I would need to take medication for the rest of my life to prevent another manic episode. At that moment I thought I had no choice but to accept this as my new reality. But God had other plans.

THE MIRACLE

I wouldn't be here writing this if it weren't for my mom. Even though she didn't fully understand what was happening to me, she stayed by my side, praying and trying to make sense of my struggles. There were times when she would lay hands on me and command the oppressive spirit to leave in Jesus' name. She spoke so much hope into my life at a time when I felt hopeless and defeated. She would tell me over and over, "You are going to be OK. This is not the rest of your life. You are going to be fine." Her encouragement and faith helped me believe I was going to be OK and reminded me that my true identity was in Christ alone.

When the doctor gave me my diagnosis, I made up my mind right then and there that I was going to be healed. I would beat this disease because I knew that if God is for me, who can be against me (Rom. 8:31)? I decided that if my mom could have such strong faith for me, I could believe too. I remembered that my words had power—a lesson my mom had instilled in us as kids—so I refused to speak the illness over my life.

My parents, my grandpa, and other strong believers in my family stood in prayer for my healing. Two weeks after I received my diagnosis and started the proper medications, my mom and I attended church one Sunday morning. As the service came to a close, the pastor and his wife invited anyone in need of prayer to come forward. My mom turned to me and said, "Dayne, you should go up for prayer." Being someone who went up to the altar for prayer only a handful of times in my entire life, I didn't hesitate to agree with her. I walked straight up to the pastor and his wife at the front of the church.

During our prayer I had a physical reaction; my hands began to shake uncontrollably, and I started making strange noises. As their prayer came to an end, I felt something physically lift off my body, and I knew beyond any shadow of a doubt that I had just been healed in the name of Jesus. I was *so* grateful for what had just happened and thanked the pastor and his wife for praying for me. They still seemed a bit startled, but I knew the healing had already taken place. As the Bible says, "For where two or three are gathered together in My name, I am there in the midst of them" (Matt. 18:20, NKJV). In that moment, I received healing through faith.

I was so thankful for their prayer that I went to speak with the pastor after the service. He seemed surprised when I approached him, and he said, "Uh, I gotta get my daughter a donut," before walking away. Though his response caught me off guard, I was filled with gratitude for the powerful way God had moved in my life. I had heard of people being miraculously healed, but I had never experienced it myself.

Shortly after that day, I stopped taking all the medication I had been prescribed. That was more than ten years ago, and I haven't needed medication for my mental health since.

THE FINAL ASSIGNMENT

After experiencing God's supernatural healing, I decided to pursue a new career in technology as I completed my final semester at ASU. I secured a position at a local tech startup and began a fresh chapter in my career. My time in technology sales blessed my life greatly. I had the opportunity to travel across the United States, working with major companies in banking, technology, and e-commerce. Throughout it all I was able to use my gift of encouragement with my colleagues. I was so thankful for what God had done in my life and how He was helping me move into this new phase.

Then the world shut down, and I was forced to work from home. I could sense the effect isolation was having on people's minds. A spirit of fear gripped our society, and all we saw in the world was darkness and death. As I was leaning heavily into the Lord during this time, I felt the Holy Spirit prompting me over and over to start sharing my faith online. Having never done anything like that, I wrestled with the call for weeks, thinking, "Lord, who am I to share my faith? I'm not qualified. I'm not a pastor. I can't. I can't. I can't." Of course, I didn't realize it at the time, but I was trying to close a door of opportunity God was opening for me because I thought I lacked the qualifications.

Ephesians 2:10 reminds us that "we are God's handiwork, created in Christ Jesus to do good works, which God prepared in advance for us to do." Jesus does not look for who is qualified; He is the One who qualifies those who are called. As I sat with the Lord each day trying to tell Him why I couldn't share my faith online, I asked Him a specific question that would change my life forever. Matthew 7:7 says, "Ask and it will be given to you; seek and you will find; knock and the door will be opened to you." So I asked God, "If You want me to share my faith, what could I share comfortably and confidently?" I sensed the answer immediately: prayer. I was to start sharing my faith by encouraging others through prayer.

This gave me permission to not overthink what sharing my faith had to look like. I didn't need to be a pastor or Bible teacher for God to use me. Though I felt a strong conviction that this was exactly how the Lord wanted me to proceed, I was still hesitant about what people might think of me. To overcome this, I decided to start sharing my faith on TikTok, a fairly new social media platform at the time where no one knew me. I wanted to be obedient to what God was asking of me, so I decided to simply post a prayer video every day. I had no expectations about what would come from it. I wasn't trying to grow a following or become a social media influencer. My goal was just to be obedient to God's call to share my faith.

I would record a short prayer video in the morning, post it, and go back to my technology job, which I loved. I did this for six to eight months. I didn't blow up on social media or have a video go viral, but the content was reaching a few thousand people each week. I got to see the difference my videos could make in people's lives during a time when fear and uncertainty gripped our world. I even started to do live streams at night where I prayed for people and shared my testimony publicly for the first time. I saw God do something I never imagined: He turned around an experience that was once so painful and used it for good. My testimony brought hope to people who were facing similar challenges in their mental health. I also received testimonies from others who had been healed. I was so encouraged and was beginning to better understand what God was using me to do.

After a year of sharing my faith online, I made another decision: to learn everything I could about using social media to better reach people. I wanted to be a good steward of what God had given me, and over the next six months my prayer videos began to reach millions of people. God was so faithful. I was beginning to see what God wanted for my future, and two years into sharing my faith online, I felt Him asking me to step away from my career to pursue this full-time.

This was the next difficult decision I had to make, because I would have to trust God enough to leave a career He had used to bless me both professionally and financially. I was making very little money as a content creator, but I remembered that God specifically asked me to trust Him. I had enough money saved up to make the leap, and after a few weeks of sitting with the Lord, I decided to leave my career behind.

The first ten months were really hard, as I worried about how I would make this work financially. But God gave me a word that helped me change my perspective. He said, "I asked you to trust Me, not focus on what's not there financially. Stop keeping your eyes on the finances, and keep your eyes fixed on Me." All the stress and worry I was experiencing were a result of what I was focusing on. God wanted me to understand that trusting Him meant focusing on Him and Him alone, not the finances. He helped me see that as I kept my eyes on Him, He would give me the peace to navigate the transition.

The peace I started to experience changed everything about how I viewed that season. In the last two months of that first year, God started to provide financially, and I started making enough to meet my needs. He proved Himself so faithful. He just wanted me to fully trust Him. It's been more than five years since that time, and God has remained faithful in every area of my life. A decision to answer His call and be obedient to Him each day has led me to what has been the most rewarding experience of my life: sharing my faith with others daily as a digital evangelist.

Chapter 2

WHAT IS PRAYER?

PRAYER IS HOW my relationship with Jesus developed, and to this day it remains one of the most important practices in my walk with God. Through prayer we have the incredible privilege of speaking directly to God. It's something anyone can do, at any age, and it's as simple or as profound as we make it. You can pray out loud or silently, formally or informally, privately or publicly. Prayer can be serious or lighthearted, filled with worship, thanksgiving, requests—whatever is on your heart. You don't need a priest, pastor, or anyone else to talk to God. Although prayer is simple, it's also the foundation of a strong Christian life because communication with God deepens our relationship with Him.

God made us for relationship. Our sinful nature separated us from Him because He is holy and perfect. But our heavenly Father loved us so much that He sent His Son, Jesus, to die on the cross to pay the penalty for our sins and bring us back into fellowship with Him. When we accept God's free gift of salvation by believing Jesus died and rose again, we not only receive eternal life (John 3:16); our spirits are made new (we are born again), and we enter into fellowship with God through His Holy Spirit, who is our helper and guide. (If you haven't accepted Jesus as your Savior, you'll find a prayer for salvation in the appendix. This is where transformation begins!)

When we get saved, we are like newborns. And just as babies need milk to grow, we need to be nourished by reading God's Word and spending time in prayer. Even though I grew up in church, had said the sinner's prayer, and had been baptized, I was in college when I began to develop a real, personal relationship with Jesus. It was God's kindness that led me to change my heart toward Him and begin to seek Him more deeply. This desire for deeper connection is a natural part of spiritual growth, and as we mature in faith, we can ask God to baptize us with His Holy Spirit, which leads to new levels of empowerment.

When the Holy Spirit fell on the believers in the Upper Room on the day of Pentecost, they began to speak in languages they hadn't learned and boldly spread the gospel. Today we have the same Holy Spirit to help us in every area of our lives, and one of the ways we get to know Him is through prayer. As we pray, we begin to sense God speaking to our inner spirit, offering us guidance, comfort, and encouragement by His Spirit.

WHEN YOU PRAY

In His Sermon on the Mount, Jesus taught His disciples to pray. We'll talk about the Lord's Prayer in a later chapter. For now, I want to focus on what He told them in Matthew 6:5–7: "*When you pray*, do not be like the hypocrites....But *when you pray*, go into your room....And *when you pray*, do not keep on babbling like pagans" (emphasis added). Notice that He didn't say *if* you pray, but *when*. God expects—and wants—us to talk to Him. Though Jesus was fully God and fully man, He still made time to connect with His Father in prayer (Matt. 14:23; Mark 6:46–47; John 6:15). If Jesus needed prayer, how much more do we?

Prayer shouldn't be a last resort when we're desperate or don't know what else to do. It should be our first response in everything. You can start your day with prayer by simply thanking God for the new day and sharing what's on your heart. The apostle Paul reminds us in Philippians 4:6–7: "Don't worry about anything; instead, pray about everything. Tell God what you need, and thank him for all he has done. Then you will experience God's peace, which exceeds anything we can understand. His peace will guard your hearts and minds as you live in Christ Jesus" (NLT).

Having a healthy prayer life means we're not just coming to God with our needs, but we're also building a relationship with Him through gratitude, praise, and honest conversation. Think about it—any close relationship requires time, effort, and patience. If our relationship with God is the most important one we'll ever have, it makes sense to give it our focused commitment.

Sometimes it might feel like you've been praying and nothing is changing or that God isn't hearing you. But in Jeremiah 29:12–13, God promises, "Then you will call upon Me and go and pray to Me, and I will listen to you. And you will seek Me and find Me, when you search for Me with all your heart" (NKJV). God is always listening. Over time I've seen how some of my unanswered prayers turned out for the best, as God worked in ways I hadn't expected. God works in mysterious ways, but His ways are always for our good.

When our prayer life becomes less about asking for things and more about spending time with God because we love Him, we start to notice His goodness everywhere. Here are just a few reasons for you to thank God every day:

- He loves you deeply (John 3:16; Rom. 5:8; Ps. 86:15).

- He has given you the Holy Spirit (Acts 2:38–39; John 14:16, 26).

- He has given you the gift of life (John 3:16; John 10:10; Matt. 7:14).

When our prayer life reaches a place where time with God matters more than what He can do for us, we experience a transformation in our spirit. We begin to bear the fruit of His Spirit—love, joy, peace, patience, kindness, goodness, self-control, gentleness, and faithfulness (Gal. 5:22–23)—because we are filled with Him.

Lamentations 3:22–23 says, "The faithful love of the LORD never ends! His mercies never cease. Great is his faithfulness; his mercies begin afresh each morning" (NLT). This is the power at work in you as you build your prayer life. When you seek the Lord in prayer with all your heart, you will find Him.

SPEAKING GOD'S WORD OVER YOUR LIFE

As I started building my prayer life, one of the most powerful practices I learned was speaking God's Word over my life. This helped me renew my mind daily, memorize Scripture, and hold on to God's promises. Speaking God's Word has an incredible ability to strengthen our faith and align us with what God says about us. Proverbs 18:21 reminds us, "Life and death are in the power of the tongue, and those who love it will eat its fruit" (HCSB). Our words have power, and everything we speak has the potential to build up our lives or tear them down.

To build this habit, I began incorporating Bible verses into my prayers, using Scripture as I talked with God. This practice not only helped me memorize verses but also grounded me in God's promises every day. Over the past fourteen years, as my relationship with God has deepened, these promises have become part of how I think because I've spoken them over and over again. The Bible encourages us to meditate on His Word day and night so we can live it out and find success (Josh. 1:8). As you spend time in the Word, find verses that speak to you, write them down, and use them as you pray about whatever you're facing.

I aim to speak God's promises over my life each day because His Word is alive and powerful (Heb. 4:12). As I believe God's Word by faith, I see these promises become a reality in my life. I rarely get sick, and I believe that's partly because I pray daily for health and thank God for healing my body and mind. I don't wait until I'm sick to pray for healing. If I don't feel well, I immediately claim total and complete healing, reminding myself of verses like Luke 10:19: "I have given you authority to trample on snakes and scorpions and to overcome all the power of the enemy; nothing will harm you." While this doesn't mean I'm literally hunting for snakes and scorpions, it reminds me that I don't need to fear the enemy. He's a defeated foe.

I also stand on Mark 11:24—"Whatever you ask for in prayer, believe that you have received it, and it will be yours"— and Ephesians 3:20, which says, "Now to him who is able to do immeasurably more than all we ask or imagine, according to his power that is at work within us." I want to walk in that power by believing, speaking, and receiving God's promises. When I'm well, I come into agreement with His Word, which says by His stripes I am healed (Isa. 53:5, NKJV), thank God for good health, and trust that He will keep me well.

Romans 8:37 tells us we are more than conquerors through Christ. Healing and victory aren't just for a select few; they're for everyone who believes. Don't let your current circumstances keep you from believing that God can heal you. I haven't yet experienced complete healing from the chronic pain I have from old sports injuries, but I still hold on to my faith in God's healing power. Some days the pain is intense; other times it's almost nonexistent. I've noticed that when I focus on speaking life and healing over my body rather than complaining, the pain lessens. It's a discipline I'm continually working on. I catch myself when I'm tempted to speak negatively about my body and instead tell the pain to leave in Jesus' name. Remember, our words have power, and everything we say brings either life or death.

This approach isn't just for physical pain; it applies to any challenge you face, whether it's anxiety, fear, or something else. Pay attention to where your mind goes and what words you speak when those feelings arise. If you can redirect your mind to God's Word and speak His promises aloud, you'll begin to experience freedom and peace.

John 8:32 says, "And you shall know the truth, and the truth shall make you free" (NKJV). God's Word is truth, and as we hold on to it, it frees us from anxious thoughts, overwhelming worries, and shame over past mistakes. God wants us to experience His presence and the love, joy, peace, and power that are the fruit of His Spirit. By praying and speaking His Word over our lives, we strengthen ourselves with the knowledge of God and take every negative thought captive, making it obedient to Christ (2 Cor. 10:5).

HINDRANCES TO EFFECTIVE PRAYER

James 5:16 says, "The earnest prayer of a righteous person has great power and produces wonderful results" (NLT). But are there hindrances that can make our prayers less effective and limit the outcome?

Let's look at the life of Jesus. When He walked the earth, Jesus was a man of prayer, and His ministry was marked by signs and wonders—miracles, healings, and deliverance for those oppressed by evil spirits. During His three-year ministry, He traveled extensively, teaching and meeting people's needs. When thousands came to hear Him without any food except five loaves of bread and two fish, Jesus prayed a prayer of thanksgiving. Through that prayer He multiplied the food, feeding over five thousand men (that number doesn't even include the women and children) and having twelve baskets of leftovers.

However, when Jesus visited His hometown of Nazareth, where people had watched Him grow up, He could only perform a few healings. Although Jesus was the Son of God and a man of prayer, the doubt and unbelief in Nazareth limited the impact of His ministry there. Unlike other places where Jesus healed everyone, "he did only a few miracles there because of their unbelief" (Matt. 13:58, NLT).

Our own doubts and unbelief can similarly limit the effectiveness of our prayers. In the Gospel of Mark we read about a man who asked Jesus' disciples to heal his son, who was tormented by evil spirits and unable to speak. The disciples couldn't help him, but when Jesus arrived, He healed the boy. Later, when the disciples asked why they couldn't minister healing, "Jesus said to them, 'Because of your unbelief...However, this kind does not go out except by prayer and fasting'" (Matt. 17:20–21, NKJV). The fasting was necessary to drive out their doubt and unbelief so they could pray in full faith.

When we pray for others, we may be filled with faith, but if the people we're praying for have fear, doubt, or unbelief, it can hinder the results. When we struggle with doubt and unbelief ourselves, we need to spend time in prayer and fasting to overcome those barriers and build up our faith. Faith is a key component of effective prayer.

PUTTING PRAYER INTO PRACTICE

Now, let's put what we've been discussing into practice. In 1 Thessalonians 5:16–18, Paul encourages us to "rejoice always, pray without ceasing, in everything give thanks; for this is the will of God in Christ Jesus for you" (NKJV). While it may seem impractical to pray 24/7, "without ceasing" reminds us to be persistent and consistent in our prayer lives. Since prayer is an opportunity to talk with God, we can be in conversation with Him throughout the day. You can simply thank God for what's happening in your life—whether out loud or in your thoughts. These small moments of prayer help you stay connected to God and deepen your relationship with Him.

Prayer shouldn't be complicated. Following are examples of how you can start praying about various issues or needs.

You can talk to God about anything.

- Lord, as I start my day, I want to talk to You about _____.

- Father, I need to share my thoughts and feelings about _____.

- God, I'm facing a challenge with _____ _____, and I need Your guidance.

- Dear God, I want to share with You my excitement about _____.

You can tell God what you need.

- Heavenly Father, today I come to You in need of _____.

- Lord Jesus, I ask for Your help and strength in dealing with _____.

- God, I lift up to You my concerns about
_____ and ask for
Your provision.

- Heavenly Father, I humbly ask for Your wisdom and discernment in handling _____
_____.

You can offer thanksgiving and praise.

- Lord, I want to thank You for _____.

- Father, I praise You for Your faithfulness in
_____.

- God, I'm grateful for _____
because it reminds me of Your goodness.

- Heavenly Father, thank You for _____.

You can speak God's Word over your life.

- Lord, Your Word says in Hebrews 13:5 that You will never leave me nor forsake me. Help me to trust in You as I face _____.

- Heavenly Father, Your promises bring me hope. Jeremiah 29:11 says You have plans to prosper me and not to harm me, plans to give me hope and a future as I navigate _____.

- God, Your Word declares in Psalm 139:14 that I am fearfully and wonderfully made. Help me to remember this truth and to walk confidently in Your love as I deal with _____.

- Father God, thank You for healing me from the top of my head to the bottom of my feet. I claim total and complete healing for _____ and tell _____ to go in Jesus' name. By Your stripes I am healed (Isa. 53:5).

Prayer is an open invitation to connect with God, offering us the chance to bring our joys, challenges, and needs before Him. By building this habit into our everyday lives, we're able to cultivate a relationship that is real and personal. Prayer doesn't have to be complicated or lengthy; it's about sharing our hearts openly, trusting that God is listening, and inviting Him into our daily experiences. Each moment we spend with God—whether a quick thank-You or a request for guidance—keeps us anchored in His love and reminds us that He is with us always.

Chapter 3

GOD'S MODEL FOR PRAYER

COUNTLESS BOOKS HAVE been written about prayer, but is there a "right" or "wrong" way to pray? Is there a model that guarantees results? At its core prayer is simply talking with your heavenly Father, who loves you deeply and cares about everything that matters to you. So why do we often hesitate to pray or feel we need to wait until something significant enough to warrant God's time comes up? I've found that many people are held back from praying because of thoughts like these:

- I haven't been good, so God won't hear me.

- I've asked before, and God didn't answer.

- I tried prayer and it didn't work for me.

- I don't know how to pray.

- I don't feel anything when I pray.

- I'm not a "super Christian"; maybe that's why nothing happens.

- Others prayed for me, but I haven't seen a change.

- I'm still struggling even though I'm praying.

- Prayer might work for others, but not for me.

- I don't have enough time to pray every day.

- I don't have enough faith when I pray.

If you've ever felt this way, you're not alone. Many people struggle with prayer, but I'm here to tell you prayer works, even in life's darkest seasons. I experienced this firsthand during my mental health crisis. God was faithful, and when I couldn't pray for myself, He answered the prayers of my family and my brothers and sisters in faith.

If you follow me on social media you know my prayer ministry reaches millions around the world, often through prayers that are under a minute—sometimes as short as thirty seconds. I believe God called me to deliver these brief, encouraging prayers to uplift those who are struggling. I receive thousands of requests from people asking me to pray for their situations. People need prayer, they want prayer, and they desire the strength that prayer brings. Yet a big part of my calling is to empower people to pray for themselves because it's impossible for me to respond to every single request. This book is my way of helping you and others gain confidence in prayer.

OLD AND NEW COVENANT PRAYERS

In the Old Testament, prayer was rooted in the Law, God's commandments and statutes. Many Christian denominations today still follow certain old covenant practices. For instance, Moses acted as the mediator between God and His people, often praying on their behalf because the people were afraid to approach God directly. He conveyed God's instructions to them, while priests performed sacrifices and rituals for the forgiveness of their sins. When Jesus came, He operated under the old covenant, fulfilling its requirements through His life and ministry.

With Jesus' death and resurrection, a new covenant, sealed by His blood, replaced the old covenant and allowed us to enter a relationship with God based on grace. Jesus became the mediator between God and man, giving us direct access to the Father through God's Word and the Holy Spirit. We no longer need a priest to intercede or offer sacrifices to cleanse us of sin; Jesus accomplished it all on the cross once and for all.

The Gospels reveal that Jesus' ministry lasted about three and a half years. Jesus frequently spent time alone in prayer, communing with His heavenly Father. When He prayed for people, His prayers were often answered instantly or within a short period of time. In Luke 11:1 a disciple asked Jesus, "Lord, teach us to pray just as John also taught his disciples" (AMP). In Matthew 6, Jesus taught His disciples not to pray like the hypocrites, who sought to be seen by others and be perceived as holy, nor to use vain repetitions like the heathens who thought their many words would cause them to be heard. He assured them that their heavenly Father already knew their needs before they asked, emphasizing that they didn't need to go on and on as if God hadn't heard them.

You might wonder, "Why pray if God already knows my needs?" God desires a two-way relationship with us, where we trust and depend on Him. Hebrews 4:16 encourages us, "So let us come boldly to the throne of our gracious God. There we will receive his mercy, and we will find grace to help us when we need it most" (NLT).

Jesus lived a perfect, sinless life and was our example to follow. Though fully God, He was also fully human during His time on earth and accomplished everything as a man, not relying on His divine power. By doing so, He demonstrated that we too can achieve great things through our relationship with God. As Philippians 2:6–8 (NLT) states:

Though he was God, he did not think of equality
with God as something to cling to. Instead, he gave
up his divine privileges; he took the humble position
of a slave and was born as a human being. When he
appeared in human form, he humbled himself in
obedience to God and died a criminal's death on a
cross.

How, then, did Jesus perform signs and wonders, heal, and
deliver if He was just a man? He showed us that a person who
walks closely with God can operate in the fullness of God's
power. Jesus emphasized this in John 14:12–14:

Very truly I tell you, whoever believes in me will do
the works I have been doing, and they will do even
greater things than these, because I am going to the
Father. And I will do whatever you ask in my name,
so that the Father may be glorified in the Son. You
may ask me for anything in my name, and I will
do it.

Now, let's look at what is commonly called the Lord's Prayer,
found in Luke 11:1–4 and Matthew 6:9–13. Jesus instructed
His disciples to pray in this manner—not necessarily with the
exact words, but with a focus on the key elements:

Our Father in heaven, hallowed be Your name. Your
kingdom come. Your will be done on earth as it is
in heaven. Give us this day our daily bread. And forgive us our debts, as we forgive our debtors. And do
not lead us into temptation, but deliver us from the
evil one. For Yours is the kingdom and the power
and the glory forever. Amen.

—MATTHEW 6:9–13, NKJV

This prayer is simple, memorable, and easy to recite, as many of us learned in childhood. But should we still use it as our model for prayer today? Jesus gave His disciples this prayer before His crucifixion, while He was still under the old covenant. As I mentioned, His death and resurrection marked the beginning of a new covenant, where salvation comes by grace through faith in Christ. This change means no more animal sacrifices and no more separation between God and His children. Jesus paid the price for our sins, making salvation available to anyone willing to accept it.

> For it is by grace you have been saved, through faith—and this is not from yourselves, it is the gift of God—not by works, so that no one can boast.
> —EPHESIANS 2:8–9

The Lord's Prayer, given before Jesus' death, doesn't contain the name of Jesus—the name "which is above every name" and at which "every knee should bow, of things in heaven, and things in earth, and things under the earth" (Phil. 2:9–10, KJV). When we pray to our heavenly Father, we do so in the authority of Jesus Christ, using His name as we ask and believe.

A CLOSER LOOK AT THE LORD'S PRAYER

I want to take a closer look at the Lord's Prayer and consider each line and how it can guide us in our own daily prayers.

> Our Father in heaven, hallowed [holy, revered, sacred, separated, or sanctified] be Your name. Your kingdom come. Your will be done on earth as it is in heaven. Give us this day our daily bread. And forgive us our debts [sins, trespasses], as we forgive our

debtors [those who have sinned or trespassed against us]. And do not lead us into temptation, but deliver us from the evil one. For Yours is the kingdom and the power and the glory forever. Amen.

—MATTHEW 6:9–13, NKJV

"Our Father in heaven, hallowed be Your name."

Begin your prayer with praise, gratitude, and reverence for your heavenly Father, who loves you deeply. By acknowledging God's position as the holy Creator, you affirm that He is your Source and will provide for all your needs. Although He is the almighty God, He is also your loving Father. Cultivating gratitude helps shift your focus away from problems and toward His goodness.

Sometimes we get so focused on our difficulties that we don't take time to reflect on what God has done for us. Even in times of challenge, reflecting on the blessings we do have can bring peace and perspective. For instance, you may be facing financial difficulty, but you still have a roof over your head and food on the table. Take time to list your blessings, from the air you breathe to the people who care for you, and you'll find countless reasons to be thankful.

You can also express your praise through music. If you play an instrument, use it as part of your prayer time, or listen to worship songs that bring you peace and draw your focus to God. King David, called a man after God's own heart (1 Sam. 13:14), used music to worship God, and his praise brought peace even to King Saul when he was troubled by evil spirits (1 Sam. 16:14–23). When you feel worried or anxious, worship can help calm your mind and uplift your spirit, as the enemy cannot stand praise directed to the Lord.

"Your kingdom come. Your will be done on earth as it is in heaven."

Pray that God's will be done on earth just as it is in heaven, where there is no sickness, lack, or strife. God's will is revealed in His Word. For instance, if you're unsure about His will for your health, Isaiah 53:5 (NKJV) promises that "by His stripes we are healed," affirming that healing is God's will. For mental health concerns, 2 Timothy 1:7 (AMP) reminds us that "God did not give us a spirit of timidity or cowardice or fear, but [He has given us a spirit] of power and of love and of sound judgment and personal discipline [abilities that result in a calm, well-balanced mind and self-control]." If you have loved ones struggling, you can personalize these prayers for them, asking for their peace and well-being.

If you're praying for someone's salvation, refer to 1 Timothy 2:3–4, which tells us "God our Savior...wants all people to be saved and to come to a knowledge of the truth." Ask God to soften their hearts and open doors for them to hear the gospel. James 1:5–6 also encourages you to ask God for wisdom in reaching out to them.

"Give us this day our daily bread."

Ask God to meet your daily needs and those of others you do not know, such as single moms in your community or missionaries serving abroad. This includes not only physical needs but also emotional and spiritual ones. Whether you're praying for yourself, a loved one, or someone in need, remember the command to love God wholeheartedly and to love your neighbor as yourself. God cares about our financial needs too, and He offers wisdom for managing our resources well. When we pray for provision, we trust Him as our provider.

We can ask God for anything that is according to His

will, which is revealed in His Word. For example, praying for wisdom or for a godly spouse is within His will, but praying for someone else's spouse to leave them and marry you instead is not. Seek to align your desires with God's heart.

"And forgive us our debts, as we forgive our debtors."

Through Jesus' sacrifice we have forgiveness for our sins. Receiving this forgiveness empowers us to forgive others, releasing any bitterness that might harm us spiritually and physically. Unforgiveness can lead to anger, anxiety, and depression, which hinder the abundant life Jesus promises. Remember, the enemy seeks to steal, kill, and destroy (John 10:10), and if he can't get your body, he'll go after your mind and emotions. The good news is that Jesus came to give you freedom and peace. Examine your heart and release any grudges, including those you hold against yourself. When negative memories resurface, remind yourself of God's forgiveness and declare freedom in the name of Jesus. Romans 8:1–2 tells us, "There is now no condemnation for those who are in Christ Jesus, because through Christ Jesus the law of the Spirit who gives life has set you free from the law of sin and death."

"And do not lead us into temptation, but deliver us from the evil one."

God doesn't tempt us, but He provides a way out when we face temptation. First Corinthians 10:13 says, "No temptation has overtaken you except such as is common to man; but God is faithful, who will not allow you to be tempted beyond what you are able, but with the temptation will also make the way of escape, that you may be able to bear it" (NKJV).

James 1:14 reminds us that "each one is tempted when he is drawn away by his own desires and enticed" (NKJV). To avoid compromising situations, seek God's wisdom and guidance. Choose to distance yourself from things that may weaken you, whether it's immoral influences or anxiety-inducing content. The Book of Proverbs offers valuable advice on avoiding situations that could lead you astray. Many people choose to read a chapter of Proverbs each day, matching the chapter number to the date, as the book conveniently has thirty-one chapters.

Pray that the Holy Spirit empowers you to resist the enemy's schemes and rely on God's strength to overcome. Put on the full armor of God (Eph. 6:10–20) so you can stand firm against the devil's tactics. With God's strength and His Word as your foundation, you can resist temptation and remain steadfast.

"For Yours is the kingdom and the power and the glory forever. Amen."

Close your prayer by thanking God for hearing you, and seal it in Jesus' name, affirming, "Amen," which means so be it.

The Lord's Prayer is a model for effective prayer that shows us how to approach God with reverence, humility, and trust. As we've explored each line, we see how Jesus taught us to align our hearts with God's will, rely on Him daily, seek forgiveness and extend it to others, and guard ourselves against temptation. By closing with praise we acknowledge His eternal kingdom, power, and glory, resting in the assurance that our prayers reach the One who reigns forever.

Chapter 4

OVERCOMING OBSTACLES TO EFFECTIVE PRAYER

FOR MOST OF my teenage years I didn't fully understand the power of prayer or how it could impact my life. I believed in Jesus, went to church every Sunday, and prayed occasionally, but my prayers were inconsistent and mostly reserved for times when I needed something from God. While there's nothing wrong with seeking God's help—He invites us to bring our needs to Him—prayer is meant to be so much more than a list of requests. It's an invitation to build a relationship, to connect deeply with our Creator.

MY TURNING POINT

My perspective on prayer shifted profoundly when I was eighteen. I made a commitment to pray every day—not just to ask for things, but to truly get to know God. I wanted to talk to Him as a friend, to invite Him into my life and to get to know Him more personally. Like any meaningful relationship, this required time, effort, and patience. I started talking to God whenever I had a free moment—in the early mornings, during my commute to college, or in quiet breaks throughout the day. My focus wasn't on getting something but on sharing my heart with Him.

This daily commitment was life-changing. As I spent more time in prayer, I began to trust God more, finding peace in knowing I could turn to Him whenever I felt overwhelmed or uncertain. Over time my prayer life became the foundation of my relationship with Him, guiding my choices, actions, and sense of peace. To this day prayer remains the essential practice that brings me closer to God.

Through this journey I learned that effective prayer is about aligning our lives with God's will, as revealed in His Word. It's rooted in faith, sincerity, and consistency, regardless of immediate outcomes. This journey transformed my life, and I'm sharing it with you with the hope that you, too, can experience the power and peace that come from a deeper connection with God through prayer.

WHAT IS AN EFFECTIVE PRAYER LIFE?

An effective prayer life isn't about receiving everything we ask for; it's rooted in aligning ourselves with God's will and seeking His presence above all else. True prayer invites us to come before God with faith, humility, and consistency, producing fruit for His glory. Jesus came to destroy the works of the devil and give us abundant life—this includes the fruit of the Spirit; provision; and physical, mental, and emotional healing.

In this chapter I share several core elements that define an effective prayer life.

Faith

Hebrews 11:6 says, "Without faith it is impossible to please God." Faith is more than a feeling; it's a confident assurance that God hears and responds to us. James 1:6–7 encourages us to "believe and not doubt" when we pray, teaching us to approach God with unwavering belief in His goodness and power. In Matthew 9:27–30, when Jesus healed two blind men, He said, "According to your faith let it be to you" (v. 29, NKJV), showing us that faith unlocks God's miraculous action.

Principle: Effective prayer requires faith that God hears us and will answer according to His will. "Faith comes by hearing, and hearing by the word of God" (Rom. 10:17, NKJV). Our faith grows as we read and hear God's Word, which helps us know His will.

Alignment with God's will

First John 5:14 assures us that if we ask "according to his will, he hears us." While it's natural to bring our desires to God, powerful prayer seeks His purposes above our own, trusting that He knows what's best for us. James 4:3 says, "When you ask, you do not receive, because you ask with wrong motives." God's will is revealed through Scripture and confirmed by the Holy Spirit. We have authority to pray His will over ourselves, our families, and our circumstances.

Principle: Effective prayer aligns with God's will, placing His purposes above our own. We know His will through Scripture and the Holy Spirit, who leads us into all truth. Remember, John 8:32 says, "You shall know the truth, and the truth shall make you free" (NKJV).

Persistence

First Thessalonians 5:17 urges us to "pray continually." Persistence in prayer isn't about nagging God but demonstrating our commitment and trust in Him. It's not about bargaining with God but standing confidently on His promises. Isaiah 43:26 reminds us to bring God's Word back to Him, not because He forgets but because it strengthens our faith in His unchanging goodness, mercy, love, and grace toward us, His children.

Principle: God values consistent, ongoing prayer that reflects our reliance on Him.

Righteousness

James 5:16 says, "The prayer of a righteous person is powerful and effective." Living aligned with God's ways opens our hearts to hear His voice more clearly and removes hindrances to prayer. Through faith in Jesus we are made righteous (having right standing with God). It is His righteousness that makes us holy, allowing us to approach God with a clean heart. Man's righteousness is as filthy rags (Isa. 64:6), but we are made righteous when we receive Jesus as our Lord and Savior.

Romans 3:22–24 tells us: "We are made right with God [righteous] by placing our faith in Jesus Christ. And this is true for everyone who believes, no matter who we are. For everyone has sinned; we all fall short of God's glorious standard. Yet God, in his grace, freely makes us right in his sight. He did this through Christ Jesus when he freed us from the penalty for our sins" (NLT).

Principle: Righteousness, through faith in Jesus, makes our prayers more effective. We are not being self-righteous, where we think we are so good, but we know He has forgiven us of all our unrighteousness and made us clean.

Humility

Second Chronicles 7:14 calls us to humble ourselves, acknowledging our need for God's guidance. Humility keeps an open line of communication with God, allowing us to fully receive God's grace. Proverbs 8:13 warns against pride, while James 4:6 promises grace to the humble. Being humble does not mean letting others walk all over you. It means knowing who you are in Christ, through whom we are empowered to live a victorious life.

Principle: Humbling ourselves before God allows us to

experience the fullness of His presence—His character, love, and power.

Forgiveness

Jesus teaches in Mark 11:25 that forgiveness is essential in prayer because holding on to bitterness can create a barrier between us and God. Forgiving others as God forgives us reflects His love and allows Him to work more freely in our lives.

God loved you so much that He sent Jesus to die for you and to forgive you of all your sins. How much more should you forgive those who have wronged you?

Peter asked Jesus, "Lord, how often should I forgive someone who sins against me? Seven times?" Jesus replied, "No, not seven times...but seventy times seven!" (Matt. 18:21–22, NLT). While forgiveness doesn't erase consequences—there are always consequences for actions, both positive and negative—it releases us from bitterness.

Principle: Forgiving others opens the way for effective prayer and frees us to experience God's grace.

Sincerity and honesty

In Matthew 6:7, Jesus warns against "babbling like pagans." Prayer isn't about fancy words; it's about coming to God sincerely. He is not looking for us to impress Him with fancy words. He sees our hearts and understands our pain. We can come as we are, pouring our hearts out to Him. Jesus had compassion for those who were suffering, and we can trust that He has the same compassion today.

Principle: God values genuine, heartfelt prayers over lengthy or repetitive words.

Thankfulness

Philippians 4:6 reminds us to present our requests "with thanksgiving." Remembering God's faithfulness strengthens our faith and helps us to focus on His goodness. The following story about the ten healed lepers Jesus healed illustrates the importance of gratitude.

> As Jesus continued on toward Jerusalem, he reached the border between Galilee and Samaria. As he entered a village there, ten men with leprosy stood at a distance, crying out, "Jesus, Master, have mercy on us!" He looked at them and said, "Go show yourselves to the priests." And as they went, they were cleansed of their leprosy.
>
> One of them, when he saw that he was healed, came back to Jesus, shouting, "Praise God!" He fell to the ground at Jesus' feet, thanking him for what he had done. This man was a Samaritan. Jesus asked, "Didn't I heal ten men? Where are the other nine? Has no one returned to give glory to God except this foreigner?" And Jesus said to the man, "Stand up and go. Your faith has healed you."
>
> —LUKE 17:11–19, NLT

Principle: Thanksgiving in prayer honors God's faithfulness and invites His peace. Approach God with gratitude for His many blessings, both large and small.

By incorporating these elements into our prayer life, we can deepen our relationship with God and experience the peace, guidance, and transformation that come from a life grounded in effective prayer.

ROADBLOCKS TO EFFECTIVE PRAYER

Even if we have a strong desire to pray, many obstacles can make it challenging to connect with God. Here are some common hurdles and practical solutions for overcoming them.

Distractions

In today's fast-paced world, distractions are everywhere, and it's easy for our minds to wander during prayer.

Solution: Find a quiet, peaceful space to pray, free from interruptions. Writing your thoughts or prayers down can help focus your mind and keep your attention on God.

Lack of time

Busy schedules can make it hard to prioritize prayer.

Solution: Set aside specific times for prayer, even if it's just a few minutes in the morning or before bed. Treat this time as a nonnegotiable appointment with God.

Not knowing what to say

Sometimes we may struggle with how to begin or what to say in prayer.

Solution: Remember, prayer is simply a conversation. Speak to God as you would a trusted friend—honestly, openly, and without formality.

Feeling unworthy

Feelings of guilt or shame can make us feel unworthy of approaching God.

Solution: Remember that God loves you deeply and wants to hear from you. Confess any sins, and know that He is ready to forgive and welcome you with open arms.

Doubt

Doubt can make us question whether God hears or cares about our prayers.

Solution: Meditate on scriptures that affirm God's attentiveness, like Jeremiah 29:12–13, which promises that He listens when we seek Him with all our heart.

Fear

Fear of judgment or rejection may hold us back from praying honestly.

Solution: Approach God with confidence, knowing that He desires a relationship with you and welcomes you with open arms. He invites you to share your heart with Him.

Lack of faith

At times we may feel like our prayers won't make a difference.

Solution: Reflect on stories of answered prayers in the Bible and in your own life—testimonies from friends, family, or church members. Each serves as a powerful reminder that God is actively working in the lives of those who trust Him. Remembering God's faithfulness can reignite your belief in the power of prayer.

Guilt

After making a mistake, guilt can keep us from coming to God.

Solution: Embrace God's grace and confess your sins. Know that He is always ready to forgive and restore you.

Routine and repetition

When prayer feels routine, it can become dull and disconnected.

Solution: Change up your approach—try writing your

prayers, keeping a prayer journal, or singing your praises to God. These methods can add depth and freshness to your time with God.

STAYING STRONG IN PRAYER

Developing a consistent, effective prayer life takes time and patience. As you face obstacles, remember that God is with you every step of the way. Building a relationship with Him through prayer is one of the most fulfilling pursuits you can have. It transforms your mind, calms your heart, and aligns you more closely with His will.

Becoming a prayer warrior doesn't require years of experience or special qualifications—it's a daily choice to make prayer a priority. You may be the only person lifting someone else up in prayer, and that role is powerful and essential. Take this responsibility seriously, knowing that your prayers can impact their lives in ways you may never fully see.

Embrace the opportunity to be a prayer warrior, grounded in faith, trust, and love for God and others. Set aside time each day to meet with Him—not just to make requests but to offer praise and gratitude. Let your prayers be filled with thankfulness, humility, and a genuine desire to know God more. As you stand in faith, remember that your prayers have the power to bring healing, strength, and hope to your life and to those you love.

Chapter 5

YOUR IDENTITY AND AUTHORITY IN CHRIST

DURING MY MENTAL health crisis, the enemy attacked two critical areas: my identity and my authority as a believer. Since I was still young in my understanding of God's Word, my grasp of who I was in Christ and how to exercise the authority He gave me was limited and shaky. This lack of clarity left me vulnerable to the lies and attacks that fed my mental health struggles. Without realizing what was happening, I retreated in fear, forgetting that fear doesn't come from the Lord but from the enemy—and that I had the power to resist it. I allowed myself to believe the lie that there was nothing I could do to change my situation and my condition was something I would just have to live with. Doctors reinforced this idea, suggesting that since there was no cure, the best I could do was manage it with medication. While I believe medication can be essential in some cases and that you should always consult with your doctor, my heart ached for a deeper, lasting solution.

When I was going through that manic episode during my battle with bipolar disorder, I experienced an intense rush of emotions and energy that made me feel completely out of control. For those unfamiliar, mania is more than just feeling energized or "up"—it's extreme. I felt invincible, as though nothing could stop me. But I was making reckless decisions, not getting adequate sleep, and acting in ways I didn't recognize as harmful. The scariest part was the delusions. My mind played tricks on me, making me believe things that weren't real—like that I had special abilities or was on a unique mission no one else understood. It was hard to separate reality from illusion, creating a dangerous situation for me and my loved ones. Looking back, I'm grateful for the friends and family who stepped in to help bring me back to reality, because at that time, I couldn't do it on my own.

My mom, a woman of strong faith, reminded me that my crisis didn't define my identity—Christ did. She encouraged me to reclaim the authority God had given me as a believer, declare I had a renewed mind, and speak healing and freedom over my life. The Bible says, "God has not given us a spirit of fear, but of power and of love and of a sound mind" (2 Tim. 1:7, NKJV). With that truth I started to rebuild my understanding of my identity, standing on God's promises and exercising the authority He gives us to overcome the enemy's attacks. Through the support of strong believers around me, fervent prayer, and the power of God's Word, I found true healing and freedom.

In this chapter I want to share the lessons I learned about our identity and the authority God has given us so you can stand strong whenever the enemy challenges these truths in your life. I also included some short prayers you can use when you need to strengthen yourself in these areas.

Let's start with identity. If I asked you to describe yourself, what would you say? You might mention your name, age, occupation, or that you're a believer. That's one way to think about it. Society often defines identity by our unique qualities, beliefs, or experiences. Before we come to know the Lord, we tend to root our identity in things we value at that time—whether it's based on relationships, accomplishments, the opinions of others, or even our mistakes and struggles.

I remember a poor choice I made when I was eighteen, right

after graduating high school, while on vacation in California. One night I drank too much with some classmates, and as a result I crashed headfirst off a bike without a helmet, with no one around to help. I don't even remember the crash—I only remember waking up in a hospital with a neck brace and doctors operating on my face. The next morning I saw myself in the mirror, bruised and bandaged with dozens of stitches. The guilt and shame from that decision haunted me for months. But as I grew in my relationship with God, I began to understand my true identity in Christ, and that moment of shame lost its grip on me. I still carry many of the scars from that accident, but now they're reminders of God's grace rather than my past mistakes.

Maybe you've experienced something similar—an incident or season that shaped how you feel about yourself. But here's the good news: God's Word, and the relationship we have with Him through Christ, brings freedom, security, and a purpose-filled life. Though the world might influence us to believe certain things about ourselves, the Bible tells us, "Do not conform to the pattern of this world, but be transformed by the renewing of your mind. Then you will be able to test and approve what God's will is—his good, pleasing and perfect will" (Rom. 12:2).

WHO YOU ARE IN CHRIST

Our true identity as believers is found in who we are in Christ, and Scripture is filled with promises to remind us of that. We're going to dive into those now. Hold on to these truths and come back to them whenever your identity is under attack, using the sample prayers to resist the enemy's lies.

You are a child of God.

> But to all who believed him and accepted him, he
> gave the right to become children of God.
> —JOHN 1:12, NLT

As a believer, you're not just anyone; you are a child of God.
That means you have a loving Father who cares for you deeply.
You belong to His family, and He takes responsibility for you,
providing protection, guidance, and unconditional love.

> *Father, thank You for adopting me as Your child.*
> *Help me live confidently, knowing I am loved, pro-*
> *tected, and cared for by You. Remind me daily that*
> *I belong to Your family. In Jesus' name, amen.*

You are a new creation.

> Therefore, if anyone is in Christ, he is a new cre-
> ation; old things have passed away; behold, all
> things have become new.
> —2 CORINTHIANS 5:17, NKJV

When you accept Christ, the old you is gone. You are made
new in Him. No matter what you've done or what's been done
to you, your past no longer defines you. You have a fresh start
because God has transformed your heart and spirit.

> *Lord, thank You for making me a new creation in*
> *Christ. My past no longer defines me, and I walk*
> *in the new life You have given me. I praise You*
> *for fresh starts and renewed hope. In Jesus' name,*
> *amen.*

You are chosen.

> But you are a chosen generation, a royal priesthood,
> a holy nation, His own special people, that you may
> proclaim the praises of Him who called you out of
> darkness into His marvelous light.
>
> —1 PETER 2:9, NKJV

God specifically chose you, just as you are. This means your life has purpose and meaning. You aren't here by accident; you're part of God's plan. He has a calling for you that no one else can fulfill. You have a royal identity in God's eyes. As part of His royal priesthood, you're set apart for a special purpose. You have direct access to God through the Holy Spirit, and you're called to represent Him in the world with dignity and honor.

> *Father, thank You for choosing me and setting me*
> *apart for Your purposes. Help me walk in the confi-*
> *dence of being handpicked by You, knowing I have*
> *a purpose in Your kingdom. In Jesus' name, amen.*

You are redeemed.

> In Him we have redemption through His blood, the
> forgiveness of sins, according to the riches of His
> grace.
>
> —EPHESIANS 1:7, NKJV

To have redemption means you've been bought back, saved from sin and death. Jesus paid the ultimate price for you, and that gives you freedom. You no longer have to live in guilt or shame, because God has made you free.

Father God, thank You for redeeming me through Your Son, Jesus Christ. I declare that I am free from guilt and shame because You have paid the price for me. I stand in the freedom You provide. In Jesus' name, amen.

You are righteous.

For He made Him who knew no sin to be sin for us, that we might become the righteousness of God in Him.

—2 CORINTHIANS 5:21, NKJV

Being righteous means you're in right standing with God, not because of anything you've done but because of what Christ did for you. You are fully accepted by God, and nothing can separate you from His love.

Heavenly Father, thank You that through Jesus, I am made righteous in Your sight. Help me to walk in that righteousness daily, knowing I am fully accepted by You. In Jesus' name, amen.

You are loved.

For I am persuaded that neither death nor life, neither angels nor principalities nor powers, neither things present nor things to come, neither height nor depth, nor any other created thing, shall be able to separate us from the love of God, which is in Christ Jesus our Lord.

—ROMANS 8:38–39, MEV

Nothing—absolutely nothing—can separate you from the love of God. Even when you feel unworthy or far from Him, His love remains constant. You are deeply, unconditionally loved every single day.

> *Father God, I thank You that nothing can separate me from Your love. Help me to rest in the assurance that I am deeply loved, highly favored, above and not beneath, the head and not the tail, no matter what I face. In Jesus' name, amen.*

You are an heir of God.

> ...and if children, then heirs—heirs of God and joint heirs with Christ, if indeed we suffer with Him, that we may also be glorified together.
> —ROMANS 8:17, NKJV

As an heir, you're entitled to all the blessings and promises of God. You have an inheritance in Christ, which means the same power and authority Jesus had is available to you. The inheritance we receive isn't just about material blessings in this world. It's about spiritual riches—things like the fruit of the Spirit, eternal life, a relationship with God, and power over sin. We are promised an eternal home with God where we will experience His glory forever.

> *Father God, thank You for making me an heir of Your promises. I claim the inheritance You have for me and walk in the authority and blessings that come with being Your child. In Jesus' name, amen.*

You are an ambassador of Christ.

> Now then, we are ambassadors for Christ, as though
> God were pleading through us: we implore you on
> Christ's behalf, be reconciled to God.
> —2 CORINTHIANS 5:20, NKJV

As a believer, you represent Christ in everything you do.
You are called to show His love, kindness, and truth to the
world. You are a reflection of His kingdom, and that's a great
calling.

> *Heavenly Father, thank You for calling me to rep-*
> *resent You. Help me to be a reflection of Your love,*
> *truth, and grace to those around me. Empower me*
> *to walk as Your ambassador for Christ. In Jesus'*
> *name, amen.*

You are a temple of the Holy Spirit.

> Or do you not know that your body is the temple of
> the Holy Spirit who is in you, whom you have from
> God, and you are not your own?
> —1 CORINTHIANS 6:19, NKJV

Your body is a temple, a dwelling place for the Holy Spirit.
That means God's presence lives inside of you. You carry
His power and wisdom wherever you go, and that's why it's
important to honor your body and soul.

> *Father God, thank You that Your Spirit dwells*
> *within me. Help me to honor You with my body*
> *and soul, knowing I carry Your presence wherever*
> *I go. In Jesus' name, amen.*

You are a light of the world.

> You are the light of the world. A city that is set on a
> hill cannot be hidden.
>
> —MATTHEW 5:14, MEV

You're called to shine in a dark world. God has placed His light inside you so others can see His goodness through your life. You have the power to influence those around you by simply living out your faith and trusting God in all you do.

Father, thank You for calling me to be a light in this world. Give me the courage to not hide who You created me to be. May the light of Your glory be represented in every place I go, removing any darkness and bringing hope. In Jesus' name, amen.

As believers we are not defined by the ups and downs of life, our failures, or the scars we carry. We're defined by the unchanging truth that we are loved, accepted, and empowered by God. When we fully understand this, we begin to live in the freedom, purpose, and authority that come with our identity in Christ.

Whenever you feel your identity is under attack, come back to these truths in God's Word and remind yourself that your worth comes from Christ alone. You are more than what you do or how you feel—you are a child of God, and that identity gives you access to His love, power, and promises.

YOUR AUTHORITY AS A BELIEVER

> Behold, I give you the authority to trample on ser-
> pents and scorpions, and over all the power of the
> enemy, and nothing shall by any means hurt you.
> —LUKE 10:19, NKJV

Once you know who you are in Christ, you can exercise the
authority you have been given in Him. Our identity defines
who we are in Christ, and our authority enables us to exercise
God's power.

Early in my Christian walk, not understanding my
authority kept me from overcoming the enemy and the
oppression I faced during my mental health crisis. However,
once I began to understand and operate in my authority, I was
able to fight back against the enemy and allow God's healing
power to work in my life. This brought freedom and supernatural healing from the spiritual warfare and mental health
struggles I was facing.

As a believer in Jesus, you have been given full authority
over the power of the enemy and every type of lie, attack, or
influence he may try to use against you. God gave you this
authority because you have an enemy—the devil—who "walks
about like a roaring lion, seeking whom he may devour" (1 Pet.
5:8, NKJV). Notice the verse says "whom he may devour." The
devil cannot devour everyone; however, when we are unaware
of our authority, we become vulnerable to his attacks and
influence.

To grasp our authority in Christ, let's start at the beginning. When God created Adam and Eve in His likeness, He
gave them authority to rule over the earth (Gen. 1:26–28).
They had dominion over every living creature in the air, sea,
and land and enjoyed everything in the Garden of Eden, with

only one rule: They could eat from any tree except the tree of the knowledge of good and evil. God warned them that disobedience would lead to death. But Satan, through the serpent, convinced Eve to eat the forbidden fruit, promising her knowledge that God supposedly was keeping from them. Deceived by Satan, Eve ate the fruit and gave some to Adam, who, though not deceived, chose to follow her. This act of disobedience introduced sin, death, and curses into the world and transferred the authority Adam and Eve had to Satan.

Romans 6:16 tells us, "Don't you realize that you become the slave of whatever you choose to obey? You can be a slave to sin, which leads to death, or you can choose to obey God, which leads to righteous living" (NLT). By choosing to obey the serpent, Adam and Eve surrendered their dominion over the earth to Satan, who used deception to take advantage of Eve's desire for power and knowledge.

Although Adam's and Eve's disobedience brought sin and death into the world, God had a plan for redemption. Just as one man, the first Adam, introduced sin to all mankind, Jesus Christ, the second Adam, came to restore our relationship with God and reclaim the authority that had been lost (Rom. 5:12–19). When we put our faith in Jesus, we receive forgiveness of sins and eternal life.

The Bible declares, "For all have sinned and fall short of the glory of God" (Rom. 3:23, NKJV), and "the wages of sin is death, but the gift of God is eternal life in Christ Jesus our Lord" (Rom. 6:23, NKJV). Hebrews 9:22 states, "Without the shedding of blood, there is no forgiveness" (NLT). And John 3:16 reminds us, "For God so loved the world that He gave His only begotten Son, that whoever believes in Him should not perish but have everlasting life" (NKJV).

Jesus fulfilled this promise. He was sent as the Savior, born through the lineage of Abraham, the father of the Jewish nation, just as God promised. Now, "if you confess with your mouth the Lord Jesus and believe in your heart that God has raised Him from the dead, you will be saved" (Rom. 10:9, NKJV). "For it is by grace you have been saved, through faith—and this is not from yourselves, it is the gift of God—not by works, so that no one can boast" (Eph. 2:8–9).

Jesus' death and resurrection brought an end to the old covenant—a system of laws and sacrifices—and established a new covenant through His ultimate sacrifice, providing forgiveness for humanity's sins once and for all.

Before Jesus performed His first recorded miracle, He was baptized in water by John, and God spoke from heaven, saying, "This is My beloved Son, in whom I am well pleased" (Matt. 3:17, NKJV). Jesus then went into the wilderness to fast for forty days and forty nights. There, Satan tempted Him in a manner similar to how he deceived Adam and Eve. First he questioned Jesus' identity: "If you are God's Son, turn these stones into bread." (See Matthew 4:3.) And Jesus responded with the Word of God: "Man shall not live by bread alone, but by every word that proceeds from the mouth of God" (Matt. 4:4, NKJV).

Next, Satan took Jesus to a high place and again questioned His identity: "If you are the Son of God, throw yourself down, so the angels will catch you." (See Matthew 4:6.) Jesus again countered with Scripture, reminding Satan, "You shall not tempt the LORD your God" (Deut. 6:16, NKJV). He told Satan who He was: the Lord his God. Finally, Satan offered Jesus the kingdoms of the world if He would bow down and worship him. This time, Jesus commanded Satan to go away, saying, "You shall worship the Lord your God, and Him only shall you serve" (Luke 4:8, NKJV). Jesus again declared His identity as the Lord God.

Unlike Adam and Eve, Jesus knew His identity and authority as the Son of God and was able to stand firm against Satan's temptations by declaring God's Word. Adam and Eve already possessed authority over the earth, but Satan deceived Eve by challenging her identity and the truthfulness of the word God had spoken. Adam, though fully aware of what God said, failed to exercise his authority to stop Eve or rebuke Satan.

Jesus demonstrated that knowing our identity and wielding the Word of God are essential to standing against the enemy. When we yield to temptation, we give Satan power. But James 4:7 tells us, "Submit yourselves to God. Resist the devil, and he will flee from you" (MEV). Strong's concordance defines *resist* as "to stand against" and "oppose."[1] When we stand firm against the enemy, exercising our authority and declaring God's Word, we have the power to command him to flee.

KNOW YOUR AUTHORITY—AND EXERCISE IT

So, exactly what authority have you been given?

You have power over the enemy.

> Behold, I give you the authority to trample on serpents and scorpions, and over all the power of the enemy, and nothing shall by any means hurt you.
> —LUKE 10:19, NKJV

God has given you authority over every scheme or lie of the enemy. You don't have to live in fear, because you have power over darkness. You can rebuke attacks on your mind, health, and circumstances in Jesus' name.

> *Father God, thank You for giving me authority over all the power of the enemy. I stand in the authority You've given me, declaring that no weapon formed against me shall prosper. In Jesus' name, amen.*

You're seated with Christ.

> ...and raised us up together, and made us sit together in the heavenly places in Christ Jesus.
> —EPHESIANS 2:6, NKJV

You're not powerless or defeated. You are seated with Christ in heavenly places, meaning you share in His authority. You can speak to situations from a position of victory, not defeat.

> *Heavenly Father, thank You that I am seated with Christ in heavenly places. Help me to live from a position of victory, knowing that I share in His authority. In Jesus' name, amen.*

You are victorious in Christ.

> But thanks be to God, who gives us the victory through our Lord Jesus Christ.
> —1 CORINTHIANS 15:57, NKJV

No matter what battles you face, you can have confidence because victory is already yours in Christ. You're not fighting for victory—you're fighting *from* a place of victory because Jesus has already won the battle for you by dying on the cross. Through His sacrifice you have the forgiveness of sins, freedom from bondage, healing, and the authority to overcome the enemy.

Father God, I thank You for the victory I have in Christ. I claim that victory over every challenge and battle I face today, knowing You have already won. In Jesus' name, amen.

You are more than a conqueror.

Yet in all these things we are more than conquerors through Him who loved us.

—ROMANS 8:37, NKJV

You are not just surviving—you are more than a conqueror through Christ. This means that in every situation, no matter how hard it seems, you can overcome with the strength and grace God has given you.

Heavenly Father, I thank You that I am more than a conqueror through Christ. No matter what comes my way, I know I can overcome by Your power and grace. In Jesus' name, amen.

You have access to God's promises.

And because of his glory and excellence, he has given us great and precious promises. These are the promises that enable you to share his divine nature and escape the world's corruption caused by human desires.

—2 PETER 1:4, NLT

God's promises are available for you to receive freely right now, and God never goes back on what He has promised. These promises give you access to experience His peace, provision, and power, enabling you to live victoriously and rise above the challenges and corruption of this world.

> *Father God, thank You for giving me access to all of Your promises. I stand on Your Word, claiming Your peace, provision, and protection over my life. In Jesus' name, amen.*

You are an overcomer.

> For every child of God defeats this evil world, and we achieve this victory through our faith. And who can win this battle against the world? Only those who believe that Jesus is the Son of God.
> —1 JOHN 5:4–5, NLT

As a believer you are born again, which means you have the power to overcome the world. You don't have to be defeated by trials or challenges, because your faith gives you the strength to rise above and overcome them.

> *Heavenly Father, I thank You that through faith in You, I am an overcomer. I declare victory over every obstacle and trial, knowing that my faith gives me strength in all I do. In Jesus' name, amen.*

You have the keys to the kingdom.

> And I will give you the keys of the kingdom of heaven, and whatever you bind on earth will be bound in heaven, and whatever you loose on earth will be loosed in heaven.
> —MATTHEW 16:19, NKJV

You've been given the keys of the kingdom, which means you have authority to bind and loose on earth what has already been bound and loosed in heaven. You can declare God's will in your life and see it come to pass.

Binding and loosing refer to the authority given by God to forbid or permit things in accordance with His will. To bind means to restrict or prohibit something, such as the works of the enemy, while to loose means to release or permit something, such as God's blessings and promises. This authority is rooted in declaring on earth what is already established in heaven, aligning your words and actions with God's Word and will.

> *Father God, thank You for giving me the keys of the kingdom. I bind anything that stands against Your will in my life and loose Your blessings over my circumstances. In Jesus' name, amen.*

You have authority to cast out demons.

> These miraculous signs will accompany those who believe: They will cast out demons in my name, and they will speak in new languages.
> —MARK 16:17, NLT

You have been given the authority to cast out demons and break the power of spiritual oppression. You are not a victim to spiritual forces—you have the power to command them to flee in Jesus' name.

> *Heavenly Father, thank You for giving me the authority to cast out any spiritual oppression or darkness from the enemy. I stand firm, knowing*

that in Your name every chain is broken. In Jesus'
name, amen.

You have authority to heal the sick.

> They will be able to handle snakes with safety, and if
> they drink anything poisonous, it won't hurt them.
> They will be able to place their hands on the sick,
> and they will be healed.
>
> —MARK 16:18, NLT

As a believer you have the God-given authority to lay hands
on the sick and see them recover. This passage also demonstrates God's supernatural protection in extraordinary circumstances, though it is not a call to test His power through
reckless actions. For example, when Paul was bitten by a ven-
omous snake while gathering firewood, he shook it off and
suffered no harm because God protected him (Acts 28:3–6).
You can pray for healing over yourself and others, trusting
that God works through your faith and can heal in His perfect way.

> *Father God, thank You for the authority to pray*
> *for healing. As I lay hands on myself and others, I*
> *declare Your healing power, believing for complete*
> *restoration. In Jesus' name, amen.*

You have boldness and access to God.

> ...in whom we have boldness and access with confi-
> dence through faith in Him.
>
> —EPHESIANS 3:12, NKJV

You can approach God with boldness and confidence. You don't have to hesitate or feel unworthy. Because of what Jesus did, you have direct access to God and can go to Him with your needs, prayers, and praise.

> *Heavenly Father, thank You for giving me boldness and direct access to You. I approach Your throne with confidence, knowing that You hear my prayers and respond. In Jesus' name, amen.*

Jesus is our example, and He knew His identity. Though He was fully God and fully man, He chose to live on earth as a man, setting aside His divine power. Through His actions He revealed the love of the Father, and He demonstrated that love through His sacrifice on the cross.

To walk in the authority you have in Him, you must know who you are in Christ and refuse to let society's labels or the devil's lies deceive or weaken you. When you accept Jesus as your Savior, you are born again as a child of God, which brings you into a new family with a new identity. As God's child you have rights and privileges given through His Word. However, you can't exercise these rights or fully enjoy these privileges if you don't know what they are.

Jesus knew the Scriptures, and even though He was God in human form, He took time to be alone to pray and commune with His heavenly Father. If Jesus prayed, we certainly must also take time to build our relationship with the Lord through prayer. To be effective as Christians, we also must study the Word and listen to Bible teaching. We live in a remarkable time when there are countless resources at our fingertips. Use them, but don't neglect finding a church that is grounded in the Word and believes in God's power to heal and perform miracles today.

As members of Christ's body we have been given authority to preach the gospel, heal the sick, cast out demons, and even raise the dead. Jesus said in John 14:12, "I tell you the truth, anyone who believes in me will do the same works I have done, and even greater works, because I am going to be with the Father" (NLT). How do we come to believe in Him so we can do the same works He did? By believing the Word of God, for John 1:1 tells us that Jesus is the Word.

My friends, know your identity, understand your authority, and use that authority to advance God's kingdom in your life and in the lives of others.

Chapter 6

PRAYING THE
WORD OF GOD

MY RELATIONSHIP WITH God began with a simple, consistent commitment to prayer. But as I delved deeper into His Word and discovered the richness of His promises, I longed to find a way to hold them close to my heart. A pivotal moment in my prayer life came when I started incorporating Scripture into my prayers. The Bible instructs us in Joshua 1:8: "Study this Book of Instruction continually. Meditate on it day and night so you will be sure to obey everything written in it. Only then will you prosper and succeed in all you do" (NLT). Applying God's Word to my prayers helped me hold on to His promises, memorize more of His truth, and align myself with who He created me to be.

God longs for you to build a deep relationship with Him, to experience His love, live a life filled with purpose, walk in freedom and wholeness, enjoy peace and joy, and ultimately spend eternity with Him. By incorporating His Word into your prayers, you align your heart with His will, strengthen your faith, and invite His promises to become a reality in every area of your life.

Throughout the Bible, both the Old and New Testaments, there are many examples of prayer. The Book of Psalms is filled with King David's prayers—prayers of praise, worship, repentance, and thanksgiving, as well as pleas for protection and victory. Psalm 23, one of the most beloved psalms, brings comfort to many who read and recite it:

> The Lord is my shepherd; I shall not want. He makes me lie down in green pastures; He leads me beside the still waters. He restores my soul; He leads me in the paths of righteousness for His name's sake. Yea, though I walk through the valley of the shadow of death, I will fear no evil; for You are with me; Your rod and Your staff, they comfort me. You prepare a table before me in the presence of my enemies; You anoint my head with oil; my cup runs over. Surely goodness and mercy shall follow me all the days of my life; and I will dwell in the house of the Lord forever.
>
> —Psalm 23:1–6, NKJV

As someone who tended sheep when he was a young man, David understood the role of a shepherd in guiding and protecting his sheep. He saw the Lord as the Shepherd of His people. Jesus is often called our "Good Shepherd" (John 10:11). When Jesus is your Shepherd, He takes good care of you, refreshes your soul, and gives you rest.

During one of the darkest seasons of my life, when I was hospitalized with bipolar 1 disorder, I felt overwhelmed by fear and loneliness, abandoned by God, and consumed by darkness and despair. I believed the enemy's lies, and in my ignorance and isolation I chose not to fight back. But even in those dark moments the Lord was watching over me. Someone I didn't know, possibly someone working at the hospital, visited my room and brought me a Bible. This person directed me to Psalm 23 and encouraged me to pray it over my life. I sat on my bed and prayed those verses. As soon as I finished, the darkness and fear seemed to leave the room and were replaced by a depth of peace I can't explain. Though my circumstances hadn't changed, God reminded me that He had never left my side and was there to comfort me when I needed Him most.

No matter how dark and frightening your valleys may seem, God is there to guide you through. He blesses you with His anointing and power and surrounds you with His mercy, goodness, and unfailing love, which will follow you all the days of your life, enabling you to remain in His presence.

Psalm 23 is a powerful passage to pray over your life whenever you're in a dark place mentally or emotionally. You can personalize it as a prayer, like this example:

> *Thank You, Jesus, that You are my Good Shepherd. You love and care for me and provide me with all I need. You give me inner peace and rest in my mind and emotions. You protect and guide me through all my challenges, especially those that threaten my health and well-being. I don't need to be afraid, because You are always with me, even in the presence of my enemies and those who come against me. You bless me with Your powerful anointing, and Your mercy, goodness, and unfailing love follow me wherever I go. I enjoy and rest in Your presence. In Jesus' name, I pray. Amen.*

This prayer is grounded in God's Word, which never returns empty. As Isaiah 55:11 says, "So is my word that goes out from my mouth: it will not return to me empty, but will accomplish what I desire and achieve the purpose for which I sent it." Praying God's Word is especially powerful when you face difficult challenges. I've said it before, but it bears repeating: God invites us to remind Him of His promises (Isa.

43:26), not because He forgets, but to remind ourselves that He is faithful to His Word.

Don't neglect praying God's Word over your life, even when times are good. In those moments, let His promises reinforce your faith and gratitude. Taking time to agree with God's promises helps you stay strong in your faith.

When I am healthy, I continue to pray God's promises of healing. When my career is flourishing, I speak His Word over my assignment. To help you practice praying God's Word, I've included example prayers for various areas. These prayers will help you hold on to His promises, memorize more of His Word, and align yourself with who He created you to be.

PRAYING GOD'S WORD OVER SPECIFIC AREAS OF YOUR LIFE

Prayer for your mental health (Ps. 91:1–2, NKJV):

Father God, You are my refuge and fortress. I thank You for protecting my mind and giving me peace in the midst of life's challenges. I rebuke any spirit of fear and declare Your peace over my life. In Jesus' name, amen.

Prayer for your healing (Isa. 53:5, NKJV; 1 Pet. 2:24, NKJV):

Thank You, Lord, that by Your stripes I was and am healed. Each stripe You suffered was for the healing of any disease, injury, and brokenness in my body and mind. Right now I speak healing over my body and my mind, from the top of my head to the bottom of my feet. I receive healing in my physical, mental, emotional, and spiritual self in Your mighty name, Jesus. Amen.

Prayer for your career and calling (Ps. 139:13–16; Jer. 29:11):

Thank You for the gift of life and for Your intentional plans for my future. Your Word says that You formed my inmost being and knit me together in my mother's womb. I praise You for creating me with such care and purpose. I trust in the plans You have for me, plans to prosper me and not to harm me, plans to give me hope and a future. Lord, I desire to know those plans more fully so I can walk in Your will and experience the peace and fulfillment You promise. Thank You for the gifts, talents, and ideas You've placed within me. Guide me in developing them for Your glory and lead me along the path that brings true joy. In Jesus' name, amen.

Prayer for your spiritual growth (2 Pet. 1:5–8):

Thank You for Your Holy Spirit, who guides me and reminds me how to live in a way that pleases You. I acknowledge that I don't always do what is right, but I am grateful for Your grace and forgiveness when I fall short. As Your Word encourages me to add to my faith goodness, knowledge, self-control, perseverance, godliness, mutual affection, and love, I ask for Your strength to grow in these areas. Help me to live a fruitful and victorious life, empowered by Your Spirit, so I may be effective and productive in my walk with You. In Jesus' name, amen.

Prayer for your finances (Deut. 8:18, NKJV):

Thank You, Jesus, for being my Savior and my God. As You continually bless me with abundance, help me to always give You the credit and be a blessing to others. You have empowered me to get wealth so I can help those less fortunate and spread the good news of Your love and salvation around the world. Help me to be faithful in what You have given me to do. In Jesus' name, amen.

Prayer for your family (1 Cor. 13:1–13):

Sometimes, Lord, family life can be challenging and stressful, but I know love is the key to overcoming these difficulties. Your Word reminds me that love is patient and kind; it does not envy or boast; it is not proud or self-seeking. Help me to love my family in this way—to be patient, kind, and not easily angered. Teach me to protect, trust, and persevere with wisdom and understanding, even in difficult moments. Guide me in offering encouragement when my loved ones feel insecure, and grant me discernment to help them when they need it. May Your perfect love bind our family together, keeping us strong, healthy, and wise. In Jesus' name, amen.

Prayer to deal with fear or anxiety (Heb. 4:12):

Father, I thank You that Your Word is actively strong and powerful, and as I speak it out loud, it transforms me inside and builds my faith in You. I receive Your Word that empowers me to overcome fear and anxiety [name your worry or fear]. Even though I feel the emotion of fear in my body and mind, I put my trust in You, knowing that I am well-equipped to handle the challenges I face today. In Jesus' name, amen.

Prayer for wisdom (Jas. 1:22–25, NKJV):

Lord, I want to prosper in everything I do. I need understanding and Your wisdom to accomplish my goals. As I grow in wisdom, help me to do what wisdom directs and not what my flesh desires. Help me to be a hearer and a doer of Your words of wisdom. In Jesus' name, amen.

There are many stories in the Bible of people who prayed and saw miracles, healings, the dead raised, and supernatural protection. At times, even some of those great men and women of God faced mental health challenges such as anxiety, depression, and suicidal despair. In a later chapter we will look at some of these stories to see how they apply to us today.

Praying God's Word not only renews your mind but also helps you internalize God's truth in your heart and opens the door for Him to move powerfully in your life.

PART II

POOR MENTAL HEALTH, MENTAL ILLNESS, AND PRAYER

Chapter 7

POOR MENTAL HEALTH VS. MENTAL ILLNESS

I FEEL FORTUNATE TO have grown up in a generation where iPhones didn't exist until I was sixteen and social media wasn't a thing until I was in college. My childhood outside of school was filled with sports, biking to friends' houses to play basketball, and swimming in the pool. When I wasn't outside—and I was outside a lot—I was likely at home, sometimes bored, lost in thought, or doing chores. Looking back, I see the value in those moments of "boredom." They gave me the space to think, imagine, and engage with the world around me without constant distractions.

It feels like that kind of childhood no longer exists. The world my generation grew up in is vastly different from the one today's youth experience. While I spent hours outdoors, disconnected from anything but my own imagination and friends, kids today are deeply connected to their screens. Simple activities like biking to a friend's house have been replaced by texting or DMing, and the precious boredom that once sparked creativity is now crowded with endless scrolling, likes, and notifications.

The challenges young people face go beyond just the lure of technology. Social media shapes their social lives, identities, and even mental health. Constant comparison, the need for validation, and the pressure to curate an online presence are daily realities that didn't exist for me growing up. It's no surprise that anxiety, depression, and loneliness are rising among adolescents. They live in a digital world that demands their attention every moment, leaving little room for the carefree exploration and downtime I took for granted.

Mental health wasn't a major topic of discussion when I was younger, yet over the past decade our society has faced an overwhelming mental health crisis. Today, issues such as severe anxiety and depression are at the forefront. There's a serious battle going on for our minds, and as believers we must recognize the critical role God's Word plays in defending us against the enemy's attacks on our minds. The Bible tells us, "Do not conform to the pattern of this world, but be transformed by the renewing of your mind. Then you will be able to test and approve what God's will is—his good, pleasing, and perfect will" (Rom. 12:2).

Mental health is a broad topic, but it is not the same as mental illness. Mental health encompasses our emotional, psychological, and social well-being. It influences how we think, behave, and feel, and even how we handle stress, make decisions, and connect with others.

Emotional well-being

This involves managing our emotions so we respond thoughtfully rather than impulsively. Jesus modeled this for us, as He experienced pain, anger, grief, and frustration, just as we do. He showed compassion to the sick and disabled, He was angry at the religious leaders who misused the temple, He wept before raising Lazarus from the dead, and He was frustrated with the disciples' lack of faith. Jesus lived as a man to experience the emotions we have as humans. During challenges, strong emotional well-being includes being resilient and having a positive outlook. However, those of us who have put our faith in Christ also have God's Word and Spirit to help us through all we face.

Psychological well-being

This relates to our sense of purpose, self-identity, personal growth, and satisfaction with life. It includes gratitude and serving others, which brings fulfillment. Knowing our identity in Christ means understanding that He created us for a purpose and has a good plan for us. His Word and Spirit empower us to live abundant lives.

Social well-being

Meaningful relationships with family and friends enrich our lives. God created us to connect with others. If you lack friendships, consider getting involved in your local church and being friendly. As part of Christ's body, each of us has a place and purpose. Ask God to reveal where you fit in, and seek opportunities to serve. We can volunteer, encourage, pray, and give to others. We are people of faith and also people who do good works to glorify God.

All of these areas contribute to balanced and resilient mental health. Our mental and physical health are intertwined, so keeping both strong is essential. Physical illness is often easier to diagnose, so how many of us pay attention to our mental well-being? We go through various moods—happy, sad, stressed, or calm—but what happens when these emotions become overwhelming?

RECOGNIZING POOR MENTAL HEALTH

Poor mental health can be a temporary or ongoing state in which you struggle with issues that affect your overall well-being. Stress, frustration, and feeling overwhelmed can be managed through relaxation, healthy lifestyle choices, counseling, and prayer. Sometimes we go through seasons that impact our mental and physical health negatively, but our heavenly Father wants to help us in every aspect of life.

Sometimes your body and mind simply need rest. Working nonstop can lead to exhaustion and create an opportunity for spiritual attack because you're in a weakened state. Remember, your body is the temple of the Holy Spirit, and taking care of it is essential for a healthy, long life. Your brain is also part of your body, and it too needs nourishment and care.

What are you feeding your body and brain? Are you tearing them down with alcohol, drugs, or smoking? Pray before you consume anything, asking the Lord if it is good for your health and well-being. If you know something isn't good for you, ask God for strength to overcome the desire for it. And if you're active in sports, take care to protect your head, because blows to the head can injure the brain and cause serious, lasting effects.

Many of us know we need to take care of our bodies, but we must remember that our brains also are part of God's temple, and we are called to be vigilant stewards of them as well.

SCRIPTURES TO STRENGTHEN YOUR MENTAL HEALTH

Good nutrition, adequate sleep, and exercise can boost our mental health, but nothing is more effective in combatting anxiety, fear, and other negative emotions than God's Word. Meditating on Scripture focuses our thoughts on God's promises rather than the uncertainties that often fuel our worries and fears, and it encourages us to release our burdens and find rest in Him. I have included a sampling of the scriptures you can turn to in order to combat common mental health challenges.

Anxiety and worry

- **Matthew 6:34:** "Therefore do not worry about tomorrow, for tomorrow will worry about itself. Each day has enough trouble of its own."

- **Philippians 4:6–7:** "Do not be anxious about anything, but in every situation, by prayer and petition, with thanksgiving, present your requests to God. And the peace of God, which transcends all understanding, will guard your hearts and your minds in Christ Jesus."

- **1 Peter 5:7:** "Cast all your anxiety on him because he cares for you."

Stress and being overwhelmed

- **Psalm 55:22:** "Cast your cares on the LORD and he will sustain you; he will never let the righteous be shaken."

- **Psalm 61:2:** "From the ends of the earth I call to you, I call as my heart grows faint; lead me to the rock that is higher than I."

- **Matthew 11:28–30:** "Come to me, all you who are weary and burdened, and I will give you rest. Take my yoke upon you and learn from me, for I am gentle and humble in heart, and you will find rest for your souls. For my yoke is easy and my burden is light."

Anger

- **Proverbs 15:1:** "A gentle answer turns away wrath, but a harsh word stirs up anger."

- **Ephesians 4:26–27:** "In your anger do not sin: Do not let the sun go down while you are still angry, and do not give the devil a foothold."

- **James 1:19–20:** "My dear brothers and sisters, take note of this: Everyone should be quick to listen, slow to speak and slow to become angry, because human anger does not produce the righteousness that God desires."

Fear

- **Psalm 23:4:** "Even though I walk through the darkest valley, I will fear no evil, for you are with me; your rod and your staff, they comfort me."

- **Isaiah 41:10:** "So do not fear, for I am with you; do not be dismayed, for I am your God. I will strengthen you and help you; I will uphold you with my righteous right hand."

- **2 Timothy 1:7:** "For the Spirit God gave us does not make us timid, but gives us power, love and self-discipline."

Sadness

- **Psalm 34:18:** "The LORD is close to the brokenhearted and saves those who are crushed in spirit."

- **Matthew 5:4:** "Blessed are those who mourn, for they will be comforted."

- **Revelation 21:4:** "'He will wipe every tear from their eyes. There will be no more death' or mourning or crying or pain, for the old order of things has passed away."

Frustration and confusion

- **Proverbs 3:5–6:** "Trust in the LORD with all your heart and lean not on your own under-standing; in all your ways submit to him, and he will make your paths straight."

- **Isaiah 26:3:** "You will keep in perfect peace those whose minds are steadfast, because they trust in you."

- **1 Corinthians 14:33:** "For God is not a God of confusion but of peace" (ESV).

Refer to these scriptures as often as you need to redirect your focus from the negative thoughts and feelings to God and His promises to give you peace and victory.

MENTAL ILLNESS

For many years mental illness was highly stigmatized and often misunderstood. Unlike general poor mental health, mental illness refers to serious, diagnosable conditions that can deeply affect one's ability to function, perception of reality, and coping mechanisms. This spectrum of disorders includes, but is not limited to, high anxiety, depression, bipolar disorder, psychosis, and schizophrenia. Effective treatment generally requires professional intervention, which may involve medication, therapy, and behavioral health support.

Recent reports from the National Alliance on Mental Illness (NAMI) and the Substance Abuse and Mental Health Services Administration (SAMHSA) reveal that approximately 1 in 5 adults in the United States—or around 57.8 million people—experience some form of mental illness each year.[1] These conditions vary widely in type and severity, from mild to life-disrupting. Among youth aged six to seventeen, 1 in 6, or roughly 16 percent, experienced mental health disorders in 2016.[2] The numbers continue to rise, especially in the areas of anxiety and depression.

The COVID-19 pandemic significantly heightened these challenges. Isolation, fear, uncertainty, and other pandemic-related stressors intensified mental health issues. According to the CDC, overdose deaths reached record levels during the pandemic as substance use increased. A 2020 CDC survey found that more than 10 percent of respondents had seriously considered suicide, with the rate highest among young people aged eighteen to twenty-four.[3]

In the face of these rising mental health challenges, it is essential that we stay hopeful. If you or a loved one struggles, take heart: There is a path to healing and wholeness. As a child of God, remember that He wants to see you healthy and healed. I share my story to encourage and remind others not to give up but to "fight the good fight of faith" (1 Tim. 6:12, NKJV). Often the greatest challenge to having good mental health is overcoming doubt and unbelief and believing God when He says He loves us and will bring us through the obstacles we face. God's healing power isn't dependent on our behavior—it's an expression of His grace. He wants you healed, and He has already made that healing available to you.

His Word is powerful and alive, and it's waiting to be activated through your faith and trust in Him.

Scriptures to Strengthen Your Faith

We overcome doubt by focusing on who God is and standing on His promises for our lives. When we immerse ourselves in His Word, our faith is strengthened, and doubt loses its grip. Following is a list of powerful scriptures to help build your faith in God's truth and eliminate doubt.

- Joshua 1:9: "Have I not commanded you? Be strong and courageous. Do not be afraid; do not be discouraged, for the LORD your God will be with you wherever you go." We must not fear or cower, because the Lord our God is with us wherever we go, giving us strength and courage to face any challenge.

- Psalm 46:10: "Be still, and know that I am God; I will be exalted among the nations, I will be exalted in the earth." This is a call to rest in the knowledge of God's sovereignty and trust in His power.

- Proverbs 3:5–6: "Trust in the LORD with all your heart and lean not on your own understanding; in all your ways submit to him, and he will make your paths straight." Faith involves trusting God's wisdom over our own, even when the path ahead is unclear.

- Isaiah 41:10: "So do not fear, for I am with you; do not be dismayed, for I am your God. I will strengthen you and help you; I will uphold you with my righteous right hand." God promises to always be with us, offering His strength in times of need.

- Matthew 17:20: "Truly I tell you, if you have faith as small as a mustard seed, you can say to this mountain, 'Move from here to there,' and it will move. Nothing will be impossible for you." You don't need a lot of faith in order to see God do incredible things. A small mustard seed grows into a huge tree. You develop mountain-moving faith as you grow in Christ. Start by trusting God to heal your minor aches and pains; then watch Him do even bigger things.

- Mark 11:24: "Therefore I tell you, whatever you ask in prayer, believe that you have received it, and it will be yours." Believing God will answer your prayer shows you trust God's faithfulness and recognize the power of prayer.

- Romans 10:17: "So then faith comes by hearing, and hearing by the word of God" (NKJV). Hearing God's Word engages us in a unique way, as it mirrors how faith was often shared and grown in biblical times—through spoken teaching and proclamation. Listening allows the Word to resonate in our hearts, stirring our faith and helping us focus, even in moments when reading might not be possible. Whether through hearing Scripture or sermons from faithful teachers, the act of listening to the Word causes it to penetrate deeply, fostering a stronger connection to God's truth.

- 2 Corinthians 5:7: "For we live by faith, not by sight." True faith means trusting God beyond what we can see or understand.

- Philippians 4:6–7: "Do not be anxious about anything, but in every situation, by prayer and petition, with thanksgiving, present your requests to God. And the peace of God, which transcends all understanding, will guard your hearts and your minds in Christ Jesus." This is how you combat worry and anxiety: Pray, and then rest in God's peace.

- Philippians 4:13: "I can do all things through Christ who strengthens me" (NKJV). Our strength comes from Christ and His anointing, not from our own abilities. This verse is not about achieving every personal dream but about relying on Christ's strength to endure and thrive in any circumstance, whether in abundance or need. When we trust in Him, we can face every challenge with confidence, knowing He is the One who sustains us.

- Hebrews 11:1: "Now faith is confidence in what we hope for and assurance about what we do not see." Faith is trusting in God's promises even when we don't yet see the results.

- James 1:3: "Because you know that the testing of your faith produces perseverance." Trials or tests are not meant to break us but to build us. They strengthen our faith, helping us to grow stronger and more resilient.

Read these scriptures, write them down, and repeat them often, personalizing each one to yourself. As you do this, work on memorizing them so they come to your mind effortlessly. When you start, you may feel uncertain, simply hoping that God's Word will work. Begin where you are; as you continue to pray and focus on what God says, your faith will grow, and doubt will diminish.

God wants you to have mental health and wholeness. During my own severe mental breakdown, I was supported by doctors, therapy, medication, and supplements providing essential nutrients. From the very beginning, even when my own prayers weren't always constant, the prayers of those around me remained steadfast. Through prayer and faith in God's grace and promises I later experienced deliverance from the demonic oppression that had gripped me. (I'll share more about that in chapter 11.) Let prayer be your first line of defense, and continue fervently until you see the full physical manifestation of your complete healing. Once you are healed, remember to thank the Lord daily for all He has done for you.

Chapter 8

HOW PRAYER AND MEDITATION AFFECT THE BRAIN

BECAUSE OF MY personal experience, I know prayer works, but that is more than just my opinion. Science has also proved the effectiveness of prayer and meditation. Studies show that prayer and meditation can positively impact brain function, emotion regulation, and overall mental well-being. While I'm not a neurologist or a researcher in that field, I'd like to share some of the fascinating insights I found while researching this subject.

Studies by neuroscientist Andrew Newberg, MD, and echoed by psychiatrist Daniel Amen, MD, demonstrate improvements in blood flow to the prefrontal cortex of the brain among people who meditate and pray regularly.[1] This increased activity in the prefrontal cortex helps improve mood and reduce anxiety. Using brain SPECT (Single Photon Emission Computed Tomography) scans, researchers have observed increases in serotonin and dopamine—two key neurotransmitters, or brain chemicals, involved in emotional and physiological regulation. These scans allow us to visibly see the areas of the brain active during prayer and meditation.[2]

The amygdala, responsible for the "fight or flight" response linked to fear and anxiety, also shows reduced activation through regular prayer, helping to lower stress and improve emotional stability. Additional studies have indicated that prayer and meditation reduce cortisol levels, a hormone associated with stress. Moreover, prayer has been shown to improve brain neuroplasticity, promoting new thought patterns that contribute to a positive outlook on life and greater resilience in coping with life's challenges.

BIBLICAL VS. WORLDLY MEDITATION

I've spoken about prayer in relation to my healing—its purpose and how to engage in it—but does meditation serve the same function as prayer? As we have discussed, at its core prayer is simply communicating with God. We are not talking to the universe, saints, or any other deity but specifically to the God of the Judeo-Christian Bible. He is the Creator of the universe—the all-knowing, all-powerful, omnipresent God who speaks to His children through the Holy Spirit, who abides within us.

With the increase in stress and anxiety, people from all religious backgrounds are being encouraged to practice some form of meditation. But there is a difference between biblical meditation and other types.

The Bible speaks of meditating on God's Word, which involves focusing on and pondering what a scripture means and asking the Holy Spirit to reveal its full significance. This kind of meditation involves not only thinking but also speaking or whispering the words—it is not a mindless chant. Unlike worldly or other religious forms of meditation, biblical meditation doesn't involve emptying the mind or detaching from life experiences; rather, it's about filling ourselves with God's Word. Practices like mindfulness meditation, transcendental meditation, yoga, and New Age meditation encourage detachment, which can inadvertently open us spiritually to unclean and unwanted demonic spirits.

Biblical meditation is active and intentional, as it involves thinking about God and what He is saying through the

Scriptures. For instance, when you read through the Psalms, you may come across the word *selah*, meaning to pause and think about what you just read. So as you read God's Word, pause and reflect on the meaning of each verse. Don't turn Bible reading into a race to check off on your to-do list; instead, ask the Holy Spirit to reveal His truth to you as you read.

The Bible speaks frequently of meditating on God and His Word:

- Joshua 1:8: "Keep this Book of the Law always on your lips; meditate on it day and night, so that you may be careful to do everything written in it. Then you will be prosperous and successful."

- Psalm 1:1–2: "Blessed is the one…whose delight is in the law of the LORD, and who meditates on his law day and night."

- Psalm 19:14: "May these words of my mouth and this meditation of my heart be pleasing in your sight, LORD, my Rock and my Redeemer."

- Psalm 63:6: "On my bed I remember you; I think of you through the watches of the night."

- Psalm 77:12: "I will consider all your works and meditate on all your mighty deeds."

- Psalm 119:15–16: "I meditate on your precepts and consider your ways. I delight in your decrees; I will not neglect your word."

- Psalm 119:97: "Oh, how I love your law! I meditate on it all day long."

- Psalm 143:5: "I remember the days of long ago; I meditate on all your works and consider what your hands have done."

- Philippians 4:8: "Finally, brothers and sisters, whatever is true, whatever is noble, whatever is right, whatever is pure, whatever is lovely, whatever is admirable—if anything is excellent or praiseworthy—think about such things."

- 1 Timothy 4:15: "Meditate on these things; give yourself entirely to them, that your progress may be evident to all" (NKJV).

Clearly, meditating on the Lord is something we should make time for as Christians.

The benefits of meditating on God's Word are beautifully illustrated in Psalm 1:3: "That person is like a tree planted by streams of water, which yields its fruit in season and whose leaf does not wither—whatever they do prospers."

Meditating on Scripture makes us like deeply rooted trees, constantly drawing nourishment from the "streams of water," which are God's Word and His teachings. This steady intake of His truth keeps us strong and steady in the midst of life's storms, and we bear good fruit in season; not just the fruit of the Spirit—love, joy, peace, patience, kindness, goodness, faithfulness, gentleness, and self-control—but other blessings as well.

Leaves that do not wither symbolize a vibrant, resilient life, able to endure winters and harsh times without losing hope or faith. And God promises that whatever you do will prosper, encompassing both spiritual and physical blessings, as we remain connected to Him by meditating on His Word.

WORRY VS. FAITH

If you've experienced worry, you know it can take over your mind and replay potential negative outcomes in what feels like a nonstop loop. In a way, worry is a type of meditation—dwelling on the worst-case scenarios that the enemy often brings to mind. Instead we're called to pray about everything and guard our hearts from trouble, as Jesus says in John 14:1: "Do not let your hearts be troubled."

If worry tends to overtake you, write down your concerns, then look up and pray through scriptures that speak hope over each worry. Remember Jesus' invitation in Matthew 11:28, "Come to me, all you who are weary and burdened, and I will give you rest."

For instance, my grandmother was a woman of prayer, but she sometimes let fear, expressed as worry, cloud her trust in God's promises. Often her concerns would come out in phrases like, "Be sure to wear something warm, or you'll get sick." She was sensitive to the Spirit, yet sometimes her emotions overrode the truth of God's Word. We can all do this, reacting with fear instead of faith. Think of times you may have felt a sore throat and thought, "Oh no, I'm getting sick," instead of speaking faith: "In Jesus' name, I reject any sickness in my body; I take authority over this symptom, and by Jesus' stripes I was and am healed right now, in Jesus' name. Amen!"

If not dealt with, worry can become a stronghold that leads to anxiety. If you struggle with excessive worry—or any other challenge—consider taking these steps to meditate on God's Word regarding your situation:

1. Find a quiet place where you can relax without distractions.

2. Tell the Lord what is on your mind and ask Him for guidance in your situation or challenge.

3. Write down the issue you're facing.

4. Look up relevant scriptures that address your need. If you're anxious, find verses that speak of peace, comfort, and healing for your mental health.

5. Write down key verses that resonate with you. Pick one, read it aloud a few times, and personalize it as a prayer.

Here is an example using the issue of anxiety.

1. Identify Bible verses that address anxiety:

- Philippians 4:6–7: "Do not be anxious about anything, but in every situation, by prayer and petition, with thanksgiving, present your requests to God. And the peace of God, which transcends all understanding, will guard your hearts and your minds in Christ Jesus."

- Matthew 6:34: "Therefore do not worry about tomorrow, for tomorrow will worry about itself. Each day has enough trouble of its own."

- 1 Peter 5:7: "Cast all your anxiety on him because he cares for you."

- Psalm 34:4: "I sought the LORD, and he answered me; he delivered me from all my fears."

- Isaiah 41:10: "So do not fear, for I am with you; do not be dismayed, for I am your God. I will strengthen you and help you; I will uphold you with my righteous right hand."

- 2 Timothy 1:7: "For God has not given us a spirit of fear, but of power and of love and of a sound mind" (NKJV).

- Proverbs 12:25: "Anxiety weighs down the heart, but a kind word cheers it up."

- John 14:27: "Peace I leave with you; my peace I give you. I do not give to you as the world gives. Do not let your hearts be troubled and do not be afraid."

- Psalm 55:22: "Cast your cares on the LORD and he will sustain you; he will never let the righteous be shaken."

- Romans 8:38–39: "For I am convinced that neither death nor life, neither angels nor demons, neither the present nor the future, nor any powers, neither height nor depth, nor anything else in all creation, will be able to separate us from the love of God that is in Christ Jesus our Lord."

2. Choose one verse and write it down, then read it aloud several times, imagining Jesus speaking this to you. For example, you could choose John 14:27: "Peace I leave with you; my peace I give you. I do not give to you as the world gives. Do not let your hearts be troubled and do not be afraid." Do this with as many verses as you like, and make it a goal to commit them to memory so you'll be able to recall them quickly whenever the enemy attacks in this area.

3. Finally, thank God for answering your prayer, saying something like, "Thank You, Jesus, for giving me Your peace, because I really need it. Help me not to be afraid and worried about what I am going through. I receive Your peace, and it's calming me down. Every time I'm anxious, please remind me that I have Your peace within me and I am not afraid."

Even if you feel pressed for time, spend a few minutes on this daily. You might choose to play praise and worship music or go outside in nature. We can meditate on God's Word anywhere—during a walk, on a run, on the drive to work—and anytime, morning or evening.

Today, as science catches up with Scripture, we know that prayer and meditating on God's Word can reduce anxiety, stress, and other mental health challenges. Unlike in worldly prayer and meditation, we are praying to the Creator of the universe, the almighty God who has all power and can orchestrate real change in our lives. It's exciting to see how medical and scientific research increasingly supports what Scripture has long taught about the impact of prayer on the mind and heart. So in times of anxiety and stress, take a moment to breathe, pray, and recall a comforting verse that invites God's peace to settle within you.

Chapter 9

BREAKING LIMITING BELIEFS AND STRONGHOLDS

THINK OF A time when something seemed out of reach—maybe it was overcoming a mental health challenge, landing your dream job, or meeting your future spouse. Despite obstacles, many of us have experienced the fulfillment of a goal that once felt impossible. What changed? Often it's because we chose to walk by faith rather than letting fear or doubt keep us from moving forward. Everything, both good and bad, begins with what we believe.

How many times have you said things like, "This is just how I am," "Things never work out for me," or, "I'll never overcome this"? These phrases often stem from fear and doubt, blocking us from all that God has for us. But where do these limiting beliefs come from? While some arise from personal experiences, they're also fueled by the enemy, whose goal is to reinforce these doubts and keep us from God's best.

Picture this: You try something new, like public speaking, but nerves get in the way. The enemy then whispers lies like, "You're not cut out for this," or, "You'll never get better at it." When these lies start to play on our doubts, they reinforce the belief that we're not capable, and so we give up trying. Over time, what began as one negative experience turns into a "truth" we accept as unchangeable: "I'm just not good at this."

The devil's goal is to distort your perception and make you believe your failures are final, you can't change, and you'll never succeed. The more you believe these lies, the more entrenched you become in a false reality where fear and doubt dictate your choices. This is the essence of deception: when a lie is repeated so often it becomes ingrained in your mind as truth. This is exactly how the devil operates—the enemy uses fear, doubt, and failure to create a cycle that keeps us trapped in insecurity and inaction.

The good news is that, just as fear and lies can create limiting beliefs, faith in God's promises can break these cycles. Instead of accepting the enemy's lies, we can choose to believe God's truth and step forward in faith. Each time we do, we see new results that help us break free from old, limiting beliefs that seek to hold us back.

The Lord says, "Fear not, for I am with you; be not dismayed, for I am your God. I will strengthen you, yes, I will help you, I will uphold you with My righteous right hand" (Isa. 41:10, NKJV). Breaking free from limiting beliefs means recognizing the enemy's lies for what they are—attempts to keep us from God's purpose—and replacing them with God's truth about who we are in Christ. With each decision to trust God and take action you create new outcomes that can build a new cycle of faith, confidence, and growth.

I remember when I first started following Jesus and was unsure how to effectively pray or connect with Him. I began by talking to Him each day, sharing my thoughts and expressing my gratitude. As I spent time in His presence, He showed me more about prayer and taught me to incorporate Scripture into my conversations with Him. This simple decision built a lasting foundation and strengthened my belief in the power of prayer. Today, I encourage others through prayer online, which I never would have imagined back then.

EXPECT OPPOSITION IN THE AREA OF YOUR CALLING

Often the areas where God wants to use us most are where we face the strongest opposition. That's why it's essential to remember our identity in Christ and the authority He's given us over all the power of the enemy. For instance, growing up, I struggled with talking to people—it was one of my biggest challenges. If you had asked me then, I would have said I'd never be comfortable speaking publicly.

As I deepened my relationship with the Lord, He began to reveal that He wanted me to pursue public speaking. So, at eighteen, I took a leap and started recording videos for YouTube. My goal wasn't to be famous; it was to obey what I felt God had placed on my heart. Even though I wasn't particularly good at it, each day I'd pick up the camera and share something I was doing or learning. For ten years I worked on developing my voice as I posted short messages online. During that time, I never gained more than five hundred subscribers. But God was preparing me for a new purpose—to share my faith online in a way I never anticipated. At twenty-eight, He called me to share messages of prayer, faith, and encouragement on social media.

Looking back, I realize that taking that first step allowed God to develop me and prepare me to step into this calling to share my faith. Don't despise small beginnings, because the Lord rejoices to see the work begin! (See Zechariah 4:10.) So if you feel called to something but face limiting beliefs, keep moving forward in faith. Trust that God is more interested in who you're becoming than in what you can achieve.

When you embrace the journey God has set before you, He will help you overcome the enemy's opposition. Through this process your mind is continually renewed by God's Word, enabling you to stay focused on your identity in Christ and confidently walk in all He has for you.

RECOGNIZE AND REPLACE LIMITING BELIEFS

In this section I want to share some common limiting beliefs, explain how the enemy uses lies to deceive us into accepting them, and show you how to use God's Word and prayer to break free. If you're struggling with any of these beliefs, I encourage you to turn to these truths whenever you feel these lies trying to hold you back.

1. Limiting belief: "I'm not good enough."

Lie from the enemy: "You'll never measure up, so why even try? You're not worthy of God's love or anyone else's."

Fight back with the truth: Ephesians 2:10 says, "For we are God's handiwork, created in Christ Jesus to do good works, which God prepared in advance for us to do."

> *Father God, thank You for creating me with purpose and value. I reject the lie that I'm not good enough, and I declare that I am Your handiwork, made for good works. Help me to walk in confidence, knowing I am loved and chosen by You. In Jesus' name, amen.*

2. Limiting belief: "I'll never be healed or set free from this."

Lie from the enemy: "Your illness, addiction, or mental health struggle will define you forever. You're stuck like this."

Fight back with the truth: Psalm 103:2–3 says, "Praise the

LORD, my soul, and forget not all his benefits—who forgives all your sins and heals all your diseases."

> *Lord God, I praise You with all my soul. I thank You for Your unending goodness and for all the benefits You've given me. You are the One who forgives all my sins and heals all my diseases. I stand on Your Word today, declaring that I am forgiven and set free. I reject the lie that my sickness or struggle defines me, and I claim Your promises of healing in my life. Thank You for being my healer, my restorer, and the One who makes me whole. In Jesus' name, amen.*

3. Limiting belief: "I don't deserve God's love."

Lie from the enemy: "Look at all your mistakes. Do you think God really loves you? You've failed too many times to be loved by God."

Fight back with the truth: Romans 8:38–39 says, "For I am convinced that neither death nor life, neither angels nor demons, neither the present nor the future, nor any powers, neither height nor depth, nor anything else in all creation, will be able to separate us from the love of God that is in Christ Jesus our Lord."

> *Heavenly Father, thank You for Your unconditional love. I reject the lie that my mistakes separate me from Your love. Help me to walk in the truth that nothing can separate me from the love You have for me in Christ Jesus. Thank You for forgiving me of my sins and helping me live a life that is pleasing to You. In Jesus' name, amen.*

4. Limiting belief: "I'm always going to struggle with anxiety/depression."

Lie from the enemy: "This is just who you are. You'll never be free from these feelings, so stop trying."

Fight back with the truth: Philippians 4:6–7 says, "Do not be anxious about anything, but in every situation, by prayer and petition, with thanksgiving, present your requests to God. And the peace of God, which transcends all understanding, will guard your hearts and your minds in Christ Jesus."

> *Father God, thank You for giving me peace that surpasses all understanding. I reject the lie that I will always be defined by these struggles, and I trust in Your promise of peace and healing. Depression and anxiety have no place in my life, and I rebuke these emotions right now in the name of Jesus. Thank You for bringing me freedom and wholeness from any mental struggles I'm facing. In Jesus' name, amen.*

5. Limiting belief: "I'll never succeed in life."

Lie from the enemy: "You're destined for failure. Others may succeed, but not you. Nothing you have ever done has succeeded, so why think any different?"

Fight back with the truth: Jeremiah 29:11 says, "'For I know the plans I have for you,' declares the Lord, 'plans to prosper you and not to harm you, plans to give you hope and a future.'"

> *Heavenly Father, I trust in Your plans for my life, Your plans to give me hope and a prosperous future. I reject the lie that I am destined to fail, and I declare that You have great plans to bless my life*

and future. Help me to walk confidently in Your
purpose for me each day. In Jesus' name, amen.

6. Limiting belief: "I can't change who I am."

Lie from the enemy: "You're stuck in your ways. No matter
how hard you try, you'll never change."

Fight back with the truth: 2 Corinthians 5:17 says,
"Therefore, if anyone is in Christ, he is a new creation; old
things have passed away; behold, all things have become new"
(NKJV).

> Father God, I thank You that in Christ, I am a new
> creation. I reject the lie that I am stuck or unable
> to change. Help me to embrace the new life You
> have given me, overcome anything holding me
> back, and walk in the transformation You bring.
> In Jesus' name, amen.

7. Limiting belief: "God doesn't have a purpose for my life."

Lie from the enemy: "You're insignificant. God's not going
to use you for anything important."

Fight back with the truth: Ephesians 1:11 says, "Because
we are united with Christ, we have received an inheritance
from God, for he chose us in advance, and he makes everything work out according to his plan" (NLT).

> Heavenly Father, thank You for choosing me and
> having a purpose for my life. Continue to reveal
> Your purpose and plan for me so that I can honor
> You with my obedience and impact those around
> me. I reject the lie that my life is insignificant, and
> I declare that I will walk in the purpose You have
> set for me. In Jesus' name, amen.

HOW LIMITING BELIEFS
BECOME STRONGHOLDS

Limiting beliefs often arise from personal experiences, inse-
curities, or fears, and are typically surface-level doubts or
assumptions about our lives. If addressed early with God's
Word, these beliefs can be overcome. But when left unad-
dressed, these beliefs can grow into something deeper—spiritual strongholds.

A stronghold, literally, is a fortified structure designed for
defense, like a military bunker or walled city. Spiritually, a
stronghold is a belief system based on a lie that contradicts
God's truth. These strongholds create entrenched thought
patterns, shaping our behaviors and perspectives as if they
were absolute truth.

After my manic episode and subsequent diagnosis I faced
two strongholds. First was the belief that I would live with
this mental health condition for the rest of my life and always
need medication to manage it. Second was the fear that my
capacity to think and learn would never be the same. These
intrusive thoughts were challenging to confront, especially as
they seemed reinforced by the doctor's diagnosis.

The struggle with my mental capacity was particularly
intense. I could tell that my mind wasn't functioning as it once
had, and I often shared my frustrations with my mom, saying
things like, "I can't remember things the way I used to," or, "It
feels like parts of my mind and intellect have been taken away
from me." I could tell that my mom and other strong believers
around me were empathetic, but they didn't accept that as the
end of the story. They knew how to stand on God's promises
and encouraged me to trust in His healing and restoration.

With their support, I began the process of tearing down

these strongholds. Embracing God's truth, I resisted the lies and continually renewed my mind according to His promises. I came to realize that I was in a spiritual battle that could only be won with spiritual weapons. These strongholds had been designed by the enemy to rob me of peace and freedom, but God had other plans.

Second Corinthians 10:3–5 reminds us: "For though we walk in the flesh, we do not war according to the flesh. For the weapons of our warfare are not carnal but mighty in God for pulling down strongholds, casting down arguments and every high thing that exalts itself against the knowledge of God, bringing every thought into captivity to the obedience of Christ" (NKJV). This passage reminds us that we aren't fighting a battle that can be won with human strength alone. Our true enemy works through lies, doubts, and deceptions—setting up mental strongholds that keep us bound in fear, confusion, or hopelessness. But God has given us spiritual weapons—His Word, prayer, and our authority in Christ—to tear these down.

By standing on God's Word, we can dismantle any lie that opposes God's truth. When faced with fear, doubt, or false beliefs about who we are or who God is, we can take each thought captive, refusing to let it control us. Every time a thought arises that contradicts God's truth, we can choose to reject it, declare His promises, and align our thinking with His Word.

This isn't just about winning a mental battle—it's about finding true freedom and peace in every area of life. As I began to embrace God's truth, I experienced supernatural healing from mental illness, freedom from medication, and complete restoration of my mind. These strongholds were broken, and what the enemy intended for harm, God turned around for good.

BREAKING STRONGHOLDS

You may be facing some challenging strongholds related to mental health or any other lie the enemy has planted in your mind, but the good news is these bondages can be broken. God has provided us with spiritual tools to tear down these barriers, and I want to help guide you through this process. Together we'll identify the lies that have taken root, replace them with God's truth, and take authority over the enemy's deception.

By the end of this chapter you'll understand not only how strongholds are formed but also how to dismantle them and experience the peace and freedom God intends for you. Just follow the four steps I outline. You don't have to stay stuck in fear, doubt, or confusion. You can have victory in Christ when you apply His Word to your life.

1. Identify the lie.

The first step is to recognize the lies that have taken root in your mind. Strongholds are built on false beliefs the enemy uses to keep us bound in fear, doubt, or confusion. So it's important to pinpoint the specific thoughts that oppose God's truth.

Ask yourself, What lies have I believed about myself, my situation, or God? Take a moment to reflect and write down these lies.

Lies:

_____

_____

2. Discover the truth.

Once the lie is identified, look to God's Word for the truth. As John 8:32 says, "And you shall know the truth, and the truth shall make you free" (NKJV). God's Word is filled with promises that expose the enemy's deception. Find scriptures that counter the lie you've been believing and write them down.

Truth:

_____

_____

3. Resist and rebuke.

James 4:7 tells us, "Submit yourselves, then, to God. Resist the devil, and he will flee from you." Resisting involves actively rejecting the lie and replacing it with God's truth.

But we don't just resist; we also rebuke—we speak against the lie and declare the truth with the authority we have been given through Christ. Jesus said in Luke 10:19, "I have given you authority to trample on snakes and scorpions and to overcome all the power of the enemy; nothing will harm you." Speak against the lie out loud and declare the truth of God's Word. Practice this daily.

Write down how you will resist and what you will rebuke in your situation.

I resist the lie that

_____

_____

I rebuke this lie in the name of Jesus and declare

_____

_____

4. Renew your mind.

The final step is to continually renew your mind with God's Word. This isn't a one-time process—it's a daily commitment. Romans 12:2 reminds us, "Do not conform to the pattern of this world, but be transformed by the renewing of your mind."

Renewing your mind means consistently replacing lies with truth, aligning your thoughts with God's promises, and allowing God's Word to reshape your perspective. This is also where repentance comes in. Repentance, or changing your mind, is about turning away from the old way of thinking and embracing God's way.

Complete this exercise by writing down a scripture that reinforces the truth, meditating on it, and declaring it over your life regularly. Then repeat this exercise for any other lies and strongholds you've been dealing with.

Scripture to meditate on:

_____

_____

Daily declaration:

_____

_____

As we have seen, limiting beliefs and strongholds start with lies rooted in our thoughts, experiences, and what we've been told. The enemy of our souls, Satan, is the father of lies and a master deceiver. But as we build our faith in the truth of God's Word, these lies lose their hold. Ask the Holy Spirit to reveal any limiting beliefs or strongholds keeping you bound. These strongholds may be causing mental anguish or despair, but the Holy Spirit is your helper, and He will empower you to break them down so you can walk in the freedom God desires for you.

Chapter 10

BIBLE HEROES WHO FACED MENTAL HEALTH CRISES

Anxiety, worry, and stress are natural responses to life's challenges, especially when we face situations beyond our control. How we react to these feelings determines whether we remain mentally strong or become overwhelmed. Although these emotions affect everyone to some extent, our ability to navigate them makes a world of difference.

In the Bible we find many examples of people who suffered from anxiety, worry, depression, and extreme stress. In this chapter we will look at a few of these biblical figures and explore their stories.

David: Anxiety and Depression

King David's journey began when he was a young shepherd tending his father's sheep. During his time in the fields, he played his harp and practiced his skill with a slingshot, which would later help him protect the flock from wild animals like lions and bears. Anointed as a teen to be Israel's future king, David gained fame by defeating the Philistine giant Goliath with just a stone and slingshot. He loved the Lord deeply and expressed his heartfelt prayers and thanksgiving in poems and songs recorded in the Book of Psalms.

Throughout his life, David faced many enemies and battled intense feelings of anxiety and depression. Though we repeatedly see him turning to God for strength, we can hear David's struggles in these verses:

> I am worn out from my groaning. All night long I
> flood my bed with weeping and drench my couch
> with tears. My eyes grow weak with sorrow; they
> fail because of all my foes.
>
> —PSALM 6:6–7

> How long must I struggle with anguish in my soul,
> with sorrow in my heart every day?
>
> —PSALM 13:2, NLT

> Be merciful to me, LORD, for I am in distress; my
> eyes grow weak with sorrow, my soul and body with
> grief. My life is consumed by anguish and my years
> by groaning; my strength fails because of my afflic-
> tion, and my bones grow weak.
>
> —PSALM 31:9–10

One of David's most distressing moments came when his men spoke of stoning him to death. While they were away, the Amalekites had raided and burned their city, Ziklag, taking all the women and children captive—including David's two wives. In anguish, David's men blamed him for leaving their families vulnerable. Despite the immense pain he was in, David found strength by turning to God. In 1 Samuel 30:6 we read that he "encouraged and strengthened himself in the LORD his God" (AMPC). David sought God's guidance, asking if he and his men should pursue the raiding party that had captured their families. God assured David that they should pursue, and he and his men would recover all. The Lord was faithful to His word. David led his men into a successful mission to rescue their families, and they recovered everyone unharmed.

In times of intense anxiety, follow David's example: Strengthen and encourage yourself in the Lord. Recall past victories and all He has done for you. Seek His counsel as Philippians 4:6–7 encourages: "Be anxious for nothing, but in everything by prayer and supplication, with thanksgiving, let your requests be made known to God; and the peace of God, which surpasses all understanding, will guard your hearts and minds through Christ Jesus" (NKJV).

For David, music and writing were vital tools for processing his feelings. Playing the harp soothed not only himself but even King Saul, who found peace when David played. When stress weighs you down, listening to praise and worship music can bring comfort to your mind and soul.

Through his writings in the Psalms we can see the depth and intimacy of David's relationship with God. Of course, David was far from perfect—he committed adultery, tried to cover up his sin, and ultimately had the woman's husband killed in battle. But he continually sought the Lord and repented sincerely when confronted with his sins. He experienced God's grace, recognizing that he deserved punishment but received mercy instead. We see this too in the Psalms—David's struggles with despair alongside his gratitude for God's goodness.

I strongly recommend you get in the habit of journaling. When you write, think of it as a personal letter to God. Use it to express your gratitude, fears, hopes—whatever you're feeling—and to identify scriptures that address your concerns. The act of writing can be deeply therapeutic, calming your mind and grounding your emotions. As you look back at your journal, you may see how God answered prayers and realize many of your worries were unfounded and that your faith has grown.

When you are feeling anxious or depressed, remember David's example. Go to God in prayer and tell Him what's on your heart.

Heavenly Father, I'm deeply troubled by [write or say your concern]. I know You love me and care for me just as You loved David. I'm so thankful that as Your child, I can come to You with anything that's heavy on my heart. You are my loving Father, and You know me better than I even know myself. Your Word says to come boldly before You and ask for grace in my time of need (Heb. 4:16). So I ask, Lord, that You give me wisdom and help me with this issue. Thank You for hearing my prayer and bringing the right outcome. In Jesus' name, I pray. Amen.

QUEEN ESTHER: ANXIETY AND EXTREME PRESSURE

Queen Esther's life was marked by courage and faith as she was used by God to save the Jewish people from annihilation. Orphaned as a child, she was raised by her relative Mordecai, a man of strong faith. Though it was known that Mordecai was a Jew, he instructed Esther to keep her Jewish identity hidden. Esther became queen of Babylon when the king, captivated by her beauty, chose her to replace the former queen, who had displeased him. Esther was given her own palace, but she could only see the king when he summoned her—approaching him without permission was punishable by death, depending on the king's mood.

Haman, the king's second-in-command, despised Mordecai, who would not bow down to him. It's possible that Mordecai refused to bow because Haman wore an idolatrous symbol forbidden by Jewish law.[1] Whatever the reason for his hatred, Haman devised a plan to have the king issue a decree to kill all Jews in the kingdom—even the elderly, women, and children.

Once signed by the king, this decree could not be undone. When Mordecai learned of this, he urged Queen Esther to go to the king and intercede for her people, but she knew that doing so could cost her life. She was under tremendous pressure and was greatly distressed.

Esther faced an agonizing choice: stay silent to protect her life or risk everything to save her people. Mordecai's words stirred her heart: Perhaps she had come to this royal position "for such a time as this"—for this very purpose (Est. 4:14). Esther asked all the Jewish people to join her and her maids in fasting from food and water for three days and nights. On the third day, she decided to approach the king, saying, "If I perish, I perish" (Est. 4:16).

In the end, God worked through Esther's bravery, turning the events around to save the Jewish people while Haman and his family suffered the very fate he had plotted for Mordecai. In times of overwhelming stress, when you may be called to do something risky or even life-threatening for the sake of others, take strength from Esther's example. Prayer and fasting invite God's power into the situation, and asking others to join you in prayer and fasting can have an incredible impact.

When I was going through my journey to recovery, my family and brothers and sisters in Christ spent time in prayer on my behalf. When you have a loved one who is suffering from a mental breakdown or disorder, prayer and fasting will help. Before fasting from food, do your research and ask the Lord for His guidance. I don't recommend fasting without water, but not eating a favorite food, skipping a meal, or abstaining from a form of entertainment or social media will help you focus on your faith to believe for healing.

I'm so thankful that I had people who loved me enough to spend time in prayer and fasting on my behalf. There were times when I was lost and thought God had abandoned me. But in those dark moments when I couldn't pray properly for myself, others were interceding for me. James 5:16 says, "The effective, fervent prayer of a righteous man avails much" (NKJV). Get in the habit of praying for others when they cross your mind or appear in your dreams—they may need your prayers. Take a few moments to lift them up in prayer; God may have placed them on your heart for a reason.

> *Heavenly Father, I'm so grateful and thankful that I can approach You with [express your need]. You are the Mighty God who knows everything and what the future holds. I pray for [say your need— healing, deliverance, finances, and so on]. Your Word says that when I pray I must believe and not doubt in my heart. Give me wisdom in this area and help me overcome doubt and unbelief. Your Word says [declare any scriptures that pertain to your request]. I believe and trust in You. Thank You for answering my prayer. In Jesus' name, amen.*

NAOMI: DEPRESSION AND HOPELESSNESS

Naomi's story is one of profound loss and despair but also of redemption and hope. She was a Jewish woman who, along with her husband and two sons, left Israel during a famine and settled in Moab, a Gentile land where the people worshipped idols. In Moab, her sons married Moabite women, which was prohibited under Jewish law. Then tragedy struck: Naomi's husband passed away, followed by both of her sons, leaving her with no support.

With nothing left in Moab, Naomi decided to return to Israel, to her family and her people. Her two daughters-in-law,

Ruth and Orpah, set out with her, but Naomi encouraged them to go back to their families and gods, freeing them to remarry and build new lives. Although Orpah returned to her family, Ruth refused to leave Naomi. She committed to staying by her side, saying that Naomi's people would become her people and that she would serve Naomi's God. Naomi, seeing Ruth's determination, accepted her company.

When Naomi and Ruth arrived in Bethlehem, there was quite a stir. The townspeople recognized Naomi and were surprised she had returned. She told them not to call her by her given name, which means "pleasant," but to call her Mara, meaning "bitter," for she believed God had dealt bitterly with her. She felt she had left Israel full, with a husband and sons, and had now returned empty and poor. Though Ruth was a loyal companion, she was also a Moabite, a Gentile and not a Jew.

Naomi was deeply depressed, grieving the loss of her family and seeing no future for herself or Ruth. With no means of support, she sent Ruth to gather leftover wheat from the fields so they could have something to eat. But even in this time of despair God was working quietly in their lives. As the story in the Book of Ruth unfolds, we see a beautiful love story take shape. Ruth meets Boaz, a wealthy and compassionate man who cares for Ruth, though she is not Jewish, and ultimately marries her. Boaz redeems Naomi's land, and he and Ruth have a son, Obed. Through Obed's descendants, the line of King David—and eventually Jesus Christ—was established in Bethlehem.

In Naomi's story we see that even in her bitterness, God had not abandoned her. He blessed her with Ruth, a loyal and loving companion who neighbors said was better to Naomi than seven sons (Ruth 4:15). Naomi's life was restored, and she found joy in caring for her grandson, Obed, as she realized that God's plan for her went far beyond her suffering.

When facing seasons of loss, it's easy to feel as Naomi did—abandoned, bitter, and hopeless. We might wonder why God allowed certain events to happen. Naomi thought God was against her, and she did not see that He had a great plan unfolding. Whatever you may be going through, hold on to hope. Like Naomi, you may find that God has a purpose beyond your present pain. When you're feeling depressed and in despair, remember Naomi's story and give your heartache to God in a prayer like this.

> *Heavenly Father, I am struggling and feeling hopeless in my situation. I don't know what to do, and I can't get out of this mess unless You help me. I depend on You. You are my answer. You are my hope. You are my deliverer because You love me so much and You have a great plan for my life (Jer. 29:11). Your Word says, "Let the weak say, 'I am strong!'" (Joel 3:10, AMP), so I say I am strong because I have Your strength and Holy Spirit within me. I thank You for Your wisdom and guidance. Fill me with Your joy because the joy of the Lord is my strength (Neh. 8:10). Thank You for bringing me out of my despair and giving me hope and joy. In Jesus' name, amen.*

BIBLE HEROES WHO FACED SUICIDAL DESPAIR

It may surprise you to learn that some champions of faith experienced moments of such intense despair that they asked God to end their lives. Though it's difficult to imagine these great men and women of God in such a low place, they were, like us, human—full of weaknesses, emotions, and doubts. Yet even in these dark times they never attempted to take their own lives, knowing that taking an innocent life—even their own—would be against God's commandments. Let's take a look at a few of these heroes who reached the point of not wanting to live and how God responded to their despair.

Moses: A burden too heavy

Moses, the remarkable leader who led the Israelites out of Egypt, witnessed God's glory, saw tremendous miracles, and even spoke with God directly. Yet he found the burden of leading an ungrateful people too much to bear. Though God had miraculously freed them from slavery, this generation of Israelites often reminisced about Egypt, seeming to forget their cries for freedom. Instead they complained to Moses, expressing frustration with the provision of manna, the heavenly food God supplied daily, and demanded meat.

The people said, "We remember the fish which we ate freely in Egypt, the cucumbers, the melons, the leeks, the onions, and the garlic" (Num. 11:5, NKJV). They seemed to overlook the harsh reality of slavery and instead focused on the foods they missed. Their complaints and lack of gratitude weighed heavily on Moses, who felt completely overwhelmed by their constant demands.

Feeling the immense pressure, Moses cried out to God: "I can't carry all these people by myself! The load is far too heavy! If this is how you intend to treat me, just go ahead and kill me. Do me a favor and spare me this misery!" (Num. 11:14–15, NLT). Moses reached his breaking point, feeling isolated and inadequate under the weight of his role.

Many of us face similar pressures—whether in leadership,

as a spouse or parent, or in caring for others. Sometimes the demands can feel unmanageable. Moses brought his heart's cry to God, and instead of answering by taking his life, God responded with provision and support. First, God sent meat in the form of quail, meeting the people's immediate demand. Then, He appointed seventy elders to share Moses' burden, filling them with His Spirit so they could help Moses lead.

God can do the same for you when you bring your heavy heart and burdens to Him. Jesus said, "Come to me, all who labor and are heavy laden, and I will give you rest" (Matt. 11:28, ESV). Scripture also says, "Cast your burden on the LORD, and he will sustain you; he will never permit the righteous to be moved" (Ps. 55:22, ESV). And Paul writes in Galatians that we are to "bear one another's burdens, and so fulfill the law of Christ" (Gal. 6:2, ESV).

If your responsibilities feel overwhelming, take them to God in prayer. Allow Him to lift your burdens, and consider sharing the load by inviting others to help. God does not expect us to carry our burdens alone.

> *Father, I thank You that I don't have to carry my burdens alone. You give me rest and provide solutions for my challenges. You said that You would sustain me when I give my burdens to You. This is my situation [describe your problem]. Show me the way and lead me to the right people who can help me resolve this. I trust You, Lord, and I don't depend on my own understanding. Give me wisdom, knowledge, understanding, and Your peace. Thank You for hearing my prayer and giving me the direction I should take. In Jesus' name, amen.*

Elijah: Fear and exhaustion

The prophet Elijah, another great leader of faith, performed extraordinary miracles through the power of God. His ministry included raising a boy from the dead, stopping the rain for three and a half years and then praying it back, and multiplying a widow's flour and oil during a famine. Elijah was even taken to heaven in a chariot of fire, making him one of only two people in the Bible who did not experience death. He fiercely preached against idolatry, confronting King Ahab and his evil wife, Jezebel, whose worship of Baal and Asherah led to widespread sin in Israel. Jezebel herself was responsible for killing many of God's prophets, and after a bold confrontation on Mount Carmel, she was determined to kill Elijah too. But I'm getting ahead of myself.

To challenge Israel's wavering faith, Elijah boldly invited Ahab to gather 450 prophets of Baal and 400 prophets of Asherah at Mount Carmel for a dramatic showdown (1 Kings 18:19). Elijah went before the Israelites and posed a powerful question: "How long will you waver between two opinions? If the LORD is God, follow him; but if Baal is God, follow him" (1 Kings 18:21).

The people said nothing. So Elijah proposed a contest. He and the prophets of Baal would each prepare a sacrifice. Then they would call on their gods, and whoever answered by fire would be recognized as the true God.

The prophets of Baal went first, calling upon their god from morning to evening to set fire to their sacrifice, yet nothing happened. Elijah even mocked them, suggesting their god might be asleep or on a trip (1 Kings 18:27). Desperate, the prophets of Baal began to cut themselves, but still no fire fell.

Finally, it was Elijah's turn. He built an altar with twelve stones representing the twelve tribes of Israel, arranged the wood, laid the sacrifice on it, and had water poured over everything until the trench around the altar overflowed. Then Elijah prayed, calling on the God of Israel to reveal His power. Instantly fire fell from heaven, consuming the sacrifice, the wood, the stones, and even the water. When the people saw it, they fell on their faces, proclaiming, "The LORD—he is God! The LORD—he is God!" (1 Kings 18:39). This was a mighty victory for God and Elijah and a powerful revelation for Israel. They saw that the gods of Baal and Asherah had no power and the God of Israel was the one true God.

When Jezebel learned her prophets had been slain, she sent word to Elijah that he would be killed within a day. Suddenly this courageous prophet of God was overcome with fear. He fled for his life, traveling over eighty miles to Beersheba. Exhausted physically, mentally, and spiritually, he collapsed under a juniper tree in the wilderness and prayed, "It is enough! Now, LORD, take my life, for I am no better than my fathers!" (1 Kings 19:4, NKJV). Despite his mighty works, Elijah was now at his breaking point, running from a death threat and asking God to take his life.

Scripture reminds us in James 5:17 that "Elijah was a man with a nature like ours [with the same physical, mental, and spiritual limitations and shortcomings]" (AMP). When a person is physically, mentally, and spiritually drained, even the most faithful can feel overwhelmed and be vulnerable to the enemy's attacks. Elijah expected Israel to repent and turn back to God after seeing such a dramatic display of His power, and when they didn't, he felt alone, discouraged, and unappreciated. But instead of turning to God for strength, Elijah allowed fear to overtake him, and he ran. Yet God in His mercy did not answer Elijah's request to die. Instead He sent an angel to provide food and water. God took care of Elijah's physical needs so he could rest and regain his strength.

As believers we must remember that everyone—even the strongest among us—will face seasons of testing, especially when we are physically or mentally drained. This underscores the importance of caring for our bodies with nourishing food, rest, and exercise, while staying close to God in prayer. We can cling to God's promises and trust Him to work in our lives. Fear is a tool of the enemy, but 2 Timothy 1:7 reminds us that "God has not given us a spirit of fear, but of power and of love and of a sound mind" (NKJV). When expectations are unmet, we may feel discouraged, but we can take comfort in knowing that "all things work together for good to those who love God, to those who are the called according to His purpose" (Rom. 8:28, NKJV).

In times of fear and exhaustion, remember that just as He was with Elijah, the Lord is with you, guiding you and working to accomplish His will.

> *Lord, thank You for giving me Your spirit of power, love, and a sound mind. I do not fear any evil because You are with me always, protecting and guiding me in all I do. Help me rest in You and be wise in caring for my physical and mental well-being. You said that You give Your beloved sleep, and I am dearly loved by You, so bless my sleep that I may awake refreshed and rested to tackle the challenges of the day. In Jesus' name, I pray. Amen.*

Jonah: Rebellion and anger

Jonah was a prophet called by God to deliver a message of impending judgment to Nineveh, a city notorious for its wickedness and an enemy of Israel. God instructed Jonah to go and warn the people of Nineveh that in forty days their city would be overthrown. But Jonah, wanting nothing to do with helping his enemies avoid destruction, instead bought a ticket on a ship bound in the opposite direction, running from God's call.

Many are familiar with the dramatic turn in Jonah's story: A fierce storm arose at sea, and Jonah confessed to the crew that it was his defiance of God that had brought the danger upon them. He urged them to throw him overboard, which they reluctantly did, and the storm subsided. God then provided a great fish to swallow Jonah, keeping him alive for three days and three nights in its belly. During this time, Jonah had time to reflect on his choices, and he repented, ultimately agreeing to follow through with God's mission. The fish released him onto dry land, and Jonah went to Nineveh to proclaim God's message of judgment.

Jonah's words struck the people of Nineveh. They believed his warning and turned to God. The king issued a decree calling everyone to fast, pray, and turn from their violent ways, hoping God would have mercy on them. True to His character, God did indeed relent and spare the city.

But rather than rejoice, Jonah was furious with God for being merciful to Israel's enemies. He confronted God, justifying his earlier attempt to flee: "Didn't I say before I left home that you would do this, LORD? That is why I ran away to Tarshish! I knew that you are a merciful and compassionate God, slow to get angry and filled with unfailing love. You are eager to turn back from destroying people. Just kill me now, LORD! I'd rather be dead than alive if what I predicted will not happen" (Jon. 4:2–3, NLT).

Jonah's anger stemmed from a heart full of bitterness toward his enemies and resentment toward God. Not only did

God spare the enemies of Israel, but Jonah also worried that he would be seen as a false prophet since the destruction he had proclaimed did not come to pass. Yet Jonah's anger toward God was misdirected. He knew that God was loving and merciful, yet he could not accept that this mercy was extended to a people he despised. His anger was so consuming that he expressed a desire to die rather than see the Ninevites spared.

Anger can be a powerful and consuming emotion, and it is sometimes even directed at God when life feels unfair or our expectations are shattered. Losing a loved one, facing rejection, enduring heartache, or grappling with failed plans can provoke anger that clouds our vision. But God's response to Jonah shows that He understands our emotions and is patient with us. He listens when we pour our hearts out to Him, even in frustration and pain.

If you find yourself in a season of anger—especially toward God—remember that He wants you to come to Him honestly. Rather than turning away, bring your hurt and anger to Him. If you've run from your calling, God is still there to bring you back. If you feel distant or overwhelmed, call on the Lord and trust that God's plans often go beyond what we can see. You might be part of His plan to bring hope and healing to others, even in the midst of your own struggles.

Heavenly Father, You are so gracious, merciful, kind, and patient with me. Help me extend to others what You have given to me because You love me so much. When I am disappointed because my prayers were not answered the way I wanted, please help me. When I am angry at You and others, help me. When I blame You for things that did not work out for me, help me.

Give me a calm and peaceful spirit as I weather the storms of life. You are my Rock, and I depend on You. Strengthen and guide me and let me only be angry at evil so that I can pray effectively. Don't let my anger turn into sin, but let me use it righteously. In Jesus' name, amen.

When you are facing trials, remember that God is always with you because His Holy Spirit lives within you. He is there guiding and sustaining you wherever you go. Nothing is too difficult for Him to handle (Jer. 32:27). In your deepest despair, call out to Him—He cares for you and loves you beyond measure. Many heroes of the Bible faced struggles they couldn't bear alone, but they cried out to God, trusting in His strength and compassion.

As 1 Corinthians 10:13 reminds us, "The temptations in your life are no different from what others experience. And God is faithful. He will not allow the temptation to be more than you can stand. When you are tempted, he will show you a way out so that you can endure" (NLT). These trials include fear, doubt, anger, and even moments of unbelief.

Your way out of despair is through the Word of God and prayer. Hold on to His promises, seek Him in prayer, and trust that He will carry you through.

PART III

THE SPIRITUAL DIMENSION OF MENTAL HEALTH

Chapter 11

THE SPIRITUAL WAR AGAINST YOUR MENTAL HEALTH

THE RISE IN mental health issues such as anxiety, depression, and other disorders has left many people struggling to cope. Some, feeling overwhelmed and hopeless, have tragically ended their lives—even young people with seemingly bright futures. Many are told there is no cure and that they'll need to rely on medication for life, supplemented by therapy to help them lead productive lives. But are medications and therapy the only options?

For those who don't know Jesus Christ as their Savior and Healer, they may seem like the only choices. However, there is promising progress in brain scan technology, which can reveal areas of the brain affected by injuries from concussions, falls, or substance abuse. Patients working with specialists in these areas may experience positive changes through lifestyle adjustments and nutritional supplementation. Some practitioners also focus on controlling toxic thought patterns and emotions to help heal the mind. Yet for me, while medical and behavioral health interventions were helpful, my complete healing came through prayer—and the ministry of deliverance.

Deliverance is a specialized area of ministry in the body of Christ that helps those who feel oppressed by unseen demonic forces. These evil spirits affect their emotions and feelings of well-being and have caused some to lose control. These people find that despite medication and therapy, they continue to struggle, and some even get worse. Those who minister deliverance rebuke these evil spirits and cast them out in the name of Jesus, exercising the spiritual authority we have been given through Christ.

A core part of Jesus' ministry involved casting out demons that were causing physical and mental illnesses in men, women, and children. The Gospels of Matthew, Mark, and Luke recount several stories of individuals being delivered from evil spirits, suggesting that many others also experienced deliverance. One remarkable account appears in Mark 5, where Jesus encounters a man in the region of the Gadarenes (also called Gerasenes) who was tormented by a demon leader named Legion because there were so many of them. This man, who was living in the tombs, cut himself with stones, cried out night and day, and had supernatural strength. When people tried to bind him, he would easily break free from the chains.

When the man approached Jesus, the demons inside him recognized Jesus and begged not to be tormented. They asked to be cast into a nearby herd of pigs, and Jesus granted their request. The demons entered about two thousand pigs, which reacted violently, running down a steep slope and drowning in the sea. The townspeople who came to see what happened found the formerly possessed man clothed and in his right mind—healed when Jesus cast the demons out of him.

In another instance, Jesus cast out seven demons from Mary Magdalene (Mark 16:9; Luke 8:2). And in yet another case, a man brought his son to Jesus because the boy was tormented by an evil spirit that would cause him to gnash his teeth, foam at the mouth, and throw himself into the fire or water (Mark 9). Jesus' disciples could not cast the demons out of the boy, but Jesus simply rebuked the evil spirit, commanding it to leave, and the man's son was cured the same hour.

The demons had no choice but to obey Jesus' command, and that same authority has been given to you and me. Before His ascension Jesus instructed His followers to do as He did—preach the gospel, heal the sick, cleanse lepers, raise the dead, and cast out demons (Mark 16:15–18).

There are some who question whether demonic influences still cause physical and mental ailments today. If so, how can we recognize when a problem is spiritual? First, we need to understand the terms *demon possession*, *demonization*, and *demonic oppression*. The King James Version uses *demon possessed*, meaning the unclean spirits are inside the person and controlling them. In the original Greek the term for this is *demonized*. Some Christians use *demonic oppression* to describe a state where a person is influenced or tormented by demonic forces but is not physically inhabited by them.

CAN CHRISTIANS BE TORMENTED BY DEMONS?

Some Christians say believers cannot be inhabited by demons because the Holy Spirit is living within them. They say a person can be lied to by the enemy and think they are being influenced by demons when it is actually their own fleshly desires warring against their spirit. Others, however, believe that while Christians cannot be "possessed," they can be oppressed by demonic influences.

Of course, there are those who seem to think there is a demon behind every ailment, and this extreme view has made some Christians avoid the area of demonic oppression. The reality is that some Christians focus too much on the demonic and not enough on the goodness of God and His power to heal. But that doesn't mean demons are not real or that they don't affect believers today. Jesus healed the sick and disabled *and* He cast out demons. Not every illness is caused by demonic forces, but some are. We need discernment from the Holy Spirit to recognize the root cause.

I have not studied the field of demonology extensively, nor do I consider myself an expert. However, based on my personal experience, I believe I was spiritually attacked by demonic forces during my mental health struggle. I am convinced that while Christians cannot be possessed—because Jesus paid the price for our salvation and our spirits are born again—evil spirits can still oppress and torment believers. The Holy Spirit dwells in Christians to help us grow in our faith. However, if we open a door to the enemy, whether through ignorance or deliberate actions, havoc can ensue. In a later chapter I will share how I believe I opened a door through my own ignorance.

Derek Prince, a man of God known for his Bible teaching and books on demonic influences, struggled with depression early in his ministry, despite praying, fasting, and reading the Bible. He eventually recognized that a spirit of depression was attacking him. One day he came across Joel 2:32, which says, "And whoever shall call on the name of the Lord shall be delivered and saved" (AMPC). He took hold of that scripture, and by doing so, he was delivered from the spirit of depression.[1]

SIGNS OF DEMONIC OPPRESSION

Signs of demonic oppression are often extreme, and though they may vary, here are a few general indicators based on the teachings of Derek Prince and others:

- Attacks during sleep: insomnia or nightmares

- Mental oppression: chronic fears; suicidal thoughts

- Controlling negative emotions: anger, hatred, violence

- Intense craving for defiled things: addictions to drugs or alcohol

- Inability to tame the tongue: chronic lying, cursing, gossip, exaggeration, impulsive actions

- Sexual perversion: involvement in pornography or sexual immorality

- Occult involvement: witchcraft; New Age practices

- Fascination with false religions: believing there are many paths to heaven

- Physical afflictions: chronic illness without a clear cause

- Compulsive behavior: impulsiveness, violent urges, compulsion to abuse one's body or engage in self-harm

- Hearing voices: experiencing tormenting or accusatory voices; multiple personalities

- Restlessness in spiritual environments: hos-
  tility toward deliverance ministers or aversion
  to prayer

- Paranormal experiences: supernatural movement of objects or animals; extreme strength

Demons are often found in packs. Resentment, unforgiveness, anger, violence, hatred, murder, disappointment,
loneliness, misery, depression, and self-destructive behavior
are usually present together. In addition, there are demons
that specifically attack the mind, namely spirits of unbelief,
doubt, compromise, forgetfulness, confusion, torment, and
insanity.

Satan's ultimate goal is to steal, kill, and destroy. As children of God we don't need to fear the supernatural realm, as
fear attracts negative and demonic forces and weakens our
faith. Some of us may be targeted by the enemy because of the
calling on our lives. Knowing the truth is crucial to exposing
demonic lies and deception.

Open doors to demonic influence include pride, rebellion,
and trauma, especially in childhood. Trauma and abuse can
leave spiritual wounds that the enemy exploits. But the good
news is that Jesus defeated the devil on the cross. As believers
we have the Holy Spirit dwelling within us and empowering
us, and He is greater than the enemy (1 John 4:4).

If you or a loved one is struggling with demonic oppression, seek God's wisdom and direction. Research deliverance ministries to ensure you are seeking help from trusted
sources. When I received prayer for deliverance, there was
no long battle to cast the demons off me. My pastors said a
prayer of faith, and I believed I would be set free. My hands
involuntarily shook, and I uttered some weird noises during

prayer, but then I felt a release and knew I was healed from that moment on. Did I recognize ahead of time that there were spiritual forces working against me? I did not, but I went up for prayer believing for healing.

I'm so thankful for God's loving-kindness and awesome grace, which are available to you too. Whether you're praying for yourself or a loved one, remember that deliverance and healing are part of the abundant life Jesus came to offer. We serve a God who is greater than any force of darkness, and He stands ready to bring freedom and peace to those who seek Him.

Chapter 12

UNDERSTANDING YOUR SPIRIT, SOUL, AND BODY

YOU AND I are human beings composed of a spirit, soul, and body. Understanding each of these parts and submitting them to God's will allows us to walk in the health, wholeness, and fullness of life Jesus died to give us. In this chapter we will take a close look at each of these three parts of our being to understand how the enemy seeks to influence us and how we can stand against him.

THE SPIRIT

When you read Genesis chapters 1 and 2, you'll see that while God created all living things, humanity was uniquely made in His image. Genesis 2:7 says God "formed man of the dust of the ground, and breathed into his nostrils the breath of life; and man became a living soul" (KJV). God's breath is what brought life to humanity's body and soul. When God breathed into man, he became alive and conscious. Although God also gave animals life, He did not breathe His Spirit into them. That distinction belongs to mankind alone, who was created to reflect God's image and likeness.

God's intent was for mankind to rule over His creation. Adam and Eve were given dominion over the earth and instructed to be fruitful and multiply. But as we've discussed, because of their disobedience Adam and Eve lost the authority they had been given, and sin entered the world. This loss of dominion was restored through Jesus Christ, whom the apostle Paul calls "the last Adam." First Corinthians 15:45

says, "The first man Adam became a living being. The last Adam became a life-giving spirit" (NKJV).

We were all born in the image of the first Adam, but when we put our faith in Christ, the last Adam, we are born again with a new spirit, capable of communicating directly with God. We become a new creation in Christ; old things have passed away, and all things are made new (2 Cor. 5:17). Our body and soul may not be new, but they conform to Christ's image as we grow in our faith. Our spirit, however, immediately becomes alive to God. We are able to worship Him in spirit and in truth because "God is a Spirit" (John 4:24, KJV).

Our human spirit is the part of us that can perceive and respond to God beyond the five senses. Proverbs 20:27 describes it this way: "The spirit of man is the candle of the Lord" (KJV). It's through our spirit that God lights our path and communicates His wisdom and direction.

Humanity's longing for spiritual connection has been evident throughout history. Unfortunately, without knowledge of the one true God, many have sought power and guidance from the spirit realm through practices like witchcraft, astrology, and fortune-telling. The same thing happens today as people embrace New Age beliefs. While they may seem harmless, these practices are contrary to God's Word and rooted in satanic deception. Satan's mission is to "steal, kill, and destroy," but Jesus came that we may have life, and have it more abundantly (John 10:10).

As I said, when you're saved, you have direct access to God because your spirit has been sanctified and made righteous through Christ. The Holy Spirit comes to dwell within you as your comforter, guide, and teacher of truth. This is a powerful truth: God's power lies within you, even though your body and soul—your flesh—may sometimes ignore your spirit's promptings. Our goal as believers is to let our spirit lead. Galatians 5:16–17 says if you "walk in the Spirit...you shall not fulfill the lust of flesh. For the flesh lusts against the Spirit, and the Spirit against the flesh; and these are contrary to one another, so that you do not do the things that you wish" (NKJV).

Your soul—mind, will, and emotions—may fluctuate, and your body may experience fatigue or illness, but your spirit, which is connected to God, remains steadfast. This is why renewing your mind with God's Word and understanding your identity in Christ are so important. Your soul must come into agreement with your reborn spirit in order for you to experience the mental and physical wholeness God desires for you (3 John 2).

As you study the Word, pray, and declare God's promises over your life, you will become more sensitive to the Holy Spirit's leading. The "natural man," who doesn't have a reborn spirit, cannot discern the things of God. But as a believer you can ask God for guidance, and His Spirit will reveal truth and guide you through your spirit (1 Cor. 2:9–16).

THE SOUL

Your soul consists of your mind, will, and emotions, and each plays a vital role in how you experience life. The mind shapes your thoughts, the will governs your choices, and emotions affect how you feel. The soul, impacted by your upbringing, experiences, and decisions, shapes your personality, and it is where God and the enemy contend for influence.

Romans 12:2 urges us, "Do not be conformed to this world, but be transformed by the renewing of your mind, that you may prove what is that good and acceptable and perfect will of God" (NKJV). Renewing your mind with God's Word is crucial because most battles we face begin in the mind, where we must choose between believing God's truth or the enemy's lies. To better illustrate this dynamic I use a framework called "Think, Do, Have":

- **Think:** Every thought we entertain shapes our perspective, influencing how we view life. Dwelling on God's promises aligns our thinking with His peace and hope, while negative thoughts can lead to stress and worry.

- **Do:** Our thoughts naturally drive our actions. When our minds are set on truth, our actions reflect trust and righteousness. Conversely, dwelling on limiting beliefs or fears can lead to hesitation or destructive behavior.

- **Have:** What we think and do determines what we experience—whether peace and joy or anxiety and turmoil. By aligning our minds and actions with God's Word, we create a life marked by peace and confidence.

Understanding this framework equips us to guard our minds, choose godly actions, and experience the freedom and peace found in Christ. Because the soul is where many mental health challenges begin, let's delve deeper into how the mind, will, and emotions work to shape our inner world.

The mind—the battle for your thoughts

Isaiah 26:3 says, "You will keep him in perfect peace, whose mind is stayed on You, because he trusts in You" (NKJV). Research suggests that the average person has around 60,000 thoughts per day, with 90 percent of them being repetitive.[1]

Some of these thoughts are positive, but many can become limiting beliefs or strongholds if they are not aligned with God's truth. You may have heard the saying, "You are what you think." I'd take it further and say you are what you believe about what you think.

While you cannot control every thought that enters your mind, you can decide which ones to dwell on. Psalm 23:3 reminds us, "He refreshes my soul. He guides me along the right paths for his name's sake." Dwelling on God's truth strengthens your soul, while entertaining lies can weaken your faith.

The mind is the front line of your soul, where you decide which thoughts to believe. Remember, "the devil walks about like a roaring lion, seeking whom he may devour" (1 Pet. 5:8, NKJV). However, he cannot devour believers who are secure in their identity in Christ. The more time you spend in God's Word, the more it shapes your thoughts and renews your mind, helping you stay grounded in His peace, protection, and abundant grace.

Your will—making godly choices

If the mind is the battlefield, the will is where victory is decided. The will is where beliefs turn into actions. Through our will, we act on our thoughts, either moving in line with God's truth or pulling away from it.

Psalm 40:8 says, "I take joy in doing your will, my God, for your instructions are written on my heart" (NLT). Like a muscle, the will can be trained and strengthened through intentional actions that reinforce God's Word. Joshua 24:15 says, "Choose for yourselves this day whom you will serve." This daily choice to serve God begins in the mind and flows through our will into actions that honor Him.

Our will often faces resistance. Temptations and distractions weaken our resolve, but again, filling our minds with God's truth equips us to overcome these challenges. Philippians 2:13 reminds us that "it is God who works in you to will and to act in order to fulfill his good purpose." Even when it's a struggle, God empowers us to make choices aligned with His purpose.

Your emotions—protecting your peace

Our emotions result from what we think and choose to do. Unlike the mind, which discerns and filters thoughts, or the will, which acts on those thoughts, our emotions are more of a reflection or byproduct of our thoughts and choices. When we align our thoughts with God's truth and direct our actions to honor Him, peace, joy, and confidence naturally follow. However, if our thoughts are clouded by fear or doubt, and our actions stray from what we know is right, our emotions often reflect anxiety, stress, or inner turmoil.

Emotions are powerful indicators of our internal state, but they're not meant to control us. Jeremiah 17:9 reminds us that "the heart is deceitful above all things," highlighting that while emotions are real, they are not always rooted in truth. Instead, emotions act as signals that reveal where our mind and will are focused. Negative emotions may indicate that we need to examine our thoughts and actions and realign them with God's Word to bring our emotions back into balance.

When our mind is renewed by God's truth and our will is guided by His Spirit, our emotions begin to reflect the fruit of the Spirit—"love, joy, peace, patience, kindness, goodness, faithfulness, gentleness, and self-control" (Gal. 5:22–23, NLT). When we center our thoughts on God's promises and choose actions that honor Him, our emotions reflect the peace and confidence that come from obeying His will.

Emotions are valuable for our growth, as they draw us closer to God. Psalm 34:17–18 reminds us that "the righteous cry out, and the LORD hears them; he delivers them from all their troubles." Emotions such as sadness and disappointment are invitations to rely on God's strength and comfort.

Because our spirit is already perfected in Christ, we must daily submit our soul—our mind, will, and emotions—to the Spirit. By doing so, we resist the temptations of the flesh, a topic we'll explore next.

THE BODY

Our bodies are a gift from God, described in Scripture as "the temple of the Holy Spirit" (1 Cor. 6:19, NKJV). This means our physical self is not only a vessel for God's presence but also a means through which we serve Him—through worship, acts of love, and discipleship. By presenting our bodies as "a living sacrifice" (Rom. 12:1), we honor God in our choices and actions.

In Scripture the term *flesh* often represents our natural, human inclinations, which can sometimes lead us away from God's purpose. Galatians 5:16–17 speaks of how our fleshly desires conflict with the Spirit, creating a tug-of-war between what we want and what God wills. These temptations of the flesh—such as instant gratification, self-centeredness, and materialism—can distract us from Christ's call. This is why it's so critical that we exercise self-control.

First John 2:16 warns about "the lust of the flesh, the lust of the eyes, and the pride of life," which are common physical desires that can lead a person away from God's will. Some examples of the works of the flesh include adultery, sexual immorality, idolatry, witchcraft, hatred, jealousy, wrath, envy, drunkenness, selfish ambition, murder, and the like (Gal.

145

5:19–21). Recognizing these temptations helps us identify areas where we may need to bring our bodies into alignment with our spiritual values.

Self-control, a fruit of the Spirit, is vital for living a disciplined life. Paul illustrates this in 1 Corinthians 9:27, where he likens self-discipline to an athlete training for a race. Practices like prayer, fasting, and healthy living strengthen us both spiritually and physically.

Just as our minds need constant renewal through God's Word, so our bodies require daily submission to the Spirit. Romans 8:12–13 reminds us not to live according to the flesh but to seek life and peace by yielding to the Spirit. Having a disciplined life in which we fill our minds with God's truth allows us to resist temptation and walk in alignment with His will.

Our physical health often reflects our spiritual condition. Stress, unresolved emotions, and fear can manifest physically. Proverbs 4:23 warns, "Above all else, guard your heart, for everything you do flows from it." By caring for our bodies through rest, nutrition, and healthy choices, we honor the life God has given us and equip ourselves to serve others and fulfill our purpose in God's kingdom.

THE CONNECTION—SPIRIT, SOUL, AND BODY

There is a dynamic connection between the spirit, soul, and body, with each part playing a unique role in our walk with God. Our spirits, made perfect and alive through Christ, connect us directly to God, empowering us to worship Him in truth and bear the fruit of the Spirit. Our souls, encompassing the mind, will, and emotions, face daily battles to choose God's truth over the enemy's lies. Finally, our bodies are the temples in which the Holy Spirit dwells, enabling us to live out our faith in the physical world.

Through the framework "Think, Do, Have" we are reminded that our thoughts shape our actions, which ultimately influence our experiences and emotions. By renewing our minds with God's Word, strengthening our will to follow His lead, and letting His truth guide our emotions, we can walk in His peace and purpose.

Caring for our bodies demonstrates our stewardship of God's gift and allows us to serve Him fully. Through obedience, self-discipline, and yielding our fleshly desires to the Spirit we honor God and submit to His purpose.

Together, the spirit, soul, and body allow us to experience the fullness of life that Jesus offers. With the tools God provides—His Word, His Spirit, and the support of others—we can guard our minds, strengthen our will, and care for our bodies, walking confidently in the freedom, peace, and strength that come from living in alignment with Him.

Chapter 13

OPENING AND CLOSING DOORS TO DEMONIC INFLUENCE

BEFORE THE MENTAL health crisis unfolded in my life, God was working powerfully in me spiritually, personally, and professionally. I was growing in the gift of encouragement and deepening my relationship with Jesus through prayer, attending church, and reading His Word. My career was thriving, and I was excelling in college. As these areas of my life flourished, I began exploring personal development books, thinking they would help me grow even more. However, as I shifted my focus toward these books, I spent less time in the Bible and began relying more on self-help principles than on God's Word. This subtle shift caused me to lower my spiritual guard, leaving a door open for the enemy to influence my thinking.

Self-help books can be valuable tools for believers to develop new skills and achieve personal growth, yet they can become a double-edged sword when we rely too heavily on them. I began to believe lies like, "You're not where you need to be"; "You're not progressing fast enough"; "The Bible is too difficult to understand"; "You need to grow faster"; "You need more tools to help you." These thoughts shifted my focus away from God and to myself. This, I believe, is one of the greatest challenges with self-help; it centers on self—your growth, your goals, and your life—often overshadowing God's foundational role in developing us into the people He created us to be.

While I remained consistent in prayer and church

attendance, I began to replace my time in God's Word with other priorities. Without realizing it, my foundation was weakening. My obsession with learning and growing masked a deeper issue: I was drifting from reliance on God's wisdom and allowing these books to take the place of His guidance. In my eagerness to grow I unknowingly created a spiritual vulnerability the enemy could exploit. Because I wasn't spending time in Scripture, I lacked the discernment to distinguish God's voice from the enemy's lies.

I started sensing a presence that I didn't understand at the time. Instead of resisting and rebuking it, I entertained it. This opened a door for the enemy to influence and oppress my life until I found myself in a state of complete mania.

Mania, or a manic state, involves heightened moods, energy, and activity levels. It's not merely excitement but a condition that can lead to impulsive actions and detachment from reality. As I've shared, this brought drastic changes in my behavior and eventually hospitalization.

What began as innocent curiosity opened the door to spiritual darkness. Thankfully, God supernaturally brought me through the darkest and most challenging experience of my life. I share this to emphasize the importance of keeping spiritual doors firmly closed to the enemy. As believers we must stand on God's Word, walk in His truth, and resist anything that sets itself up against the knowledge of Christ. As 2 Corinthians 10:4–5 reminds us, "For the weapons of our warfare are not carnal but mighty in God for pulling down strongholds, casting down arguments and every high thing that exalts itself against the knowledge of God, bringing every thought into captivity to the obedience of Christ" (NKJV).

God has given us powerful spiritual weapons to fight our mental health battles—not physical tools but divine resources capable of demolishing strongholds and silencing the enemy's lies. We must actively take every thought captive, align it with God's truth, and make it obedient to Christ. This requires resisting anything that challenges God's wisdom, standing firm in faith, and using His Word to overcome the enemy's attacks.

Let's examine some of the common ways spiritual doors are opened to the enemy—and how we can keep them firmly shut.

OPEN DOOR 1: WHAT YOU LISTEN TO

I begin with this door because it was a significant factor in the spiritual attack I faced. As I mentioned previously, my lack of time spent in God's Word left me unable to discern between God's truth and the enemy's lies. Romans 10:17 says, "So then faith comes by hearing, and hearing by the word of God" (NKJV). Reading God's Word daily strengthens our faith and equips us to recognize truth and reject deception.

We must also be mindful of the voices we allow into our lives—whether through music, TV, social media, or people we respect or admire. These influences shape our thoughts, emotions, and actions, drawing us closer to or farther from God. In my case, an overemphasis on self-help books drew me away from spending time in Scripture, creating a vulnerability in my understanding of truth versus lies. Proverbs 2:2 says to "tune your ears to wisdom, and concentrate on understanding" (NLT). The more we stay tuned to God's Word and the more He reveals the wisdom we need to navigate life's challenges, the more equipped we are to discern the truth and remain anchored in God's purpose.

Closing the door

Use this exercise to take an honest account of what you listen to each day.

1. List what you listen to on a daily basis.
   - Music (specific genres, artists, or songs)
   - Podcasts, audio content
   - TV shows, movies, YouTube videos
   - Conversations with friends, family, and coworkers
   - Social media

2. Reflect on its impact.
   - Is what I listen to impacting me positively?
   - Is it helping me grow in my faith?
   - Is there any specific message, word, or tone that feels negative, harmful, or ungodly?

3. Commit to change.
   - What negative influences do you need to reduce or eliminate?
   - How will you hold yourself accountable for this change?
   - What will you do instead of listening to this?

4. Reflect prayerfully.

   Ask God to reveal any hidden influences in what you listen to that may be hindering your spiritual growth.

Father God, help me to discern what is influencing me, and show me anything that is not leading me closer to You. Guide me in protecting my ears in a way that brings me peace, joy, and in closer alignment with Your will for my life. In Jesus' name, amen.

OPEN DOOR 2: WHAT YOU WATCH

Just like what we listen to, what we watch has a profound impact on our well-being. The psalmist declared, "I will set nothing wicked before my eyes; I hate the work of those who fall away; it shall not cling to me" (Ps. 101:3, NKJV). Consider how watching a scary movie can disrupt your sleep or cause nightmares. Similarly, the media we consume doesn't just affect us in the moment; it shapes our thoughts, attitudes, and beliefs over time, often without us realizing it.

Social media can be a great tool for connection, but it can also spread division, hate, negativity, and comparison. You may have discovered me on social media, and that's great. But it's critical to assess whether the content you consume builds your faith or fosters fear, doubt, and distraction. What you watch will either shape you into the person God designed you to be or lead you astray by the enemy's lies. Proverbs 4:23 says, "Guard your heart above all else, for it determines the course of your life" (NLT).

Closing the door

Use this exercise to take an honest account of the things you watch each day.

1. List what you watch on a daily basis.
   - TV shows or movies
   - YouTube channels or streaming content
   - Social media feeds or influencers' accounts

- News programs, documentaries, or informational content
- Any other visual media

2. Reflect on its impact.
   - Is what I watch impacting me positively?
   - Is it helping me grow in my faith?
   - Does it contain a message, word, or tone that feels negative, harmful, or worldly?

3. Commit to changing.
   - What negative influences do you need to reduce or eliminate?
   - How will you hold yourself accountable for this change?
   - What will you do instead of watching this program or content?

4. Reflect prayerfully.
   Ask God to reveal any hidden influences in what you watch that may be hindering your spiritual growth.

Heavenly Father, help me to clearly discern anything I watch that is not beneficial to my walk with You. Reveal anything that may be influencing me negatively, and guide me to focus on what is true, pure, and life-giving. In Jesus' name, amen.

Open Door 3: What You Speak

This is my favorite open door to discuss because our words are within our control. We can't always control what we see and hear, but we always choose what we say. Proverbs 18:21 reminds us that "death and life are in the power of the tongue, and those who love it will eat its fruit" (NKJV). Our words hold the power to build up or tear down, so we must choose them wisely. James 3:8–9 says, "But no one can tame the tongue. It is restless and evil, full of deadly poison. Sometimes it praises our Lord and Father, and sometimes it curses those who have been made in the image of God" (NLT). This is an important reminder that our words can be either destructive or a source of praise to God that also benefits others.

What we speak often reflects the state of our minds, influenced by what we dwell on. Philippians 4:8 urges us to think on things that are true, noble, lovely, right, admirable and praiseworthy. This is why renewing our minds with God's Word each day is so crucial, because our words will either align with God's promises, bringing life and truth, or they will reflect the enemy's lies. Just as what we watch and hear affects our minds, our words have the power to influence our hearts and shape our perspective.

Joshua 1:8 says: "This Book of the Law shall not depart from your mouth, but you shall meditate in it day and night, that you may observe to do according to all that is written in it. For then you will make your way prosperous, and then you will have good success" (NKJV). Notice the passage mentions the mouth, emphasizing the power of what we speak. Make it a daily practice to speak what the Bible says is true, not just what you feel. This is how you fight negative thoughts with life-giving truth.

If you struggle with anger, pay attention to what you say. Often when we're frustrated, our words can be harsh or hurtful because that's how we're feeling inside. As James 1:19 reminds us, "Everyone should be quick to listen, slow to speak and slow to become angry." This wisdom encourages us to pause and listen before speaking so we can avoid saying something we might regret. When you catch yourself speaking in anger, take a moment to reflect on whether your words align with God's truth or are feeding the enemy's lies. By slowing down and renewing your mind in God's Word, you'll find it easier to respond in a way that honors Him.

If you struggle with fear or anxiety, again, pay attention to the words you're speaking over yourself. When we speak out of fear, we can unintentionally agree with lies that keep a particular door open. Philippians 4:6–7 encourages, "Do not be anxious about anything, but in every situation, by prayer and petition, with thanksgiving, present your requests to God. And the peace of God, which transcends all understanding, will guard your hearts and your minds in Christ Jesus." When you catch yourself speaking words filled with fear or doubt, pause and ask God if they align with His promises. By replacing those words with His truth, you invite His peace to take root and guard your heart and mind.

Closing the door

Use this exercise to take a closer look at the impact your words are having and how you can align your speech with God's truth.

1. Reflect on the words you use each day.
   - About yourself, your friends, family, and coworkers
   - About your past, present, and future
   - On social media feeds
   - During challenging or stressful situations

2. Reflect on the impact of your words by asking
   yourself:

   - Do my words reflect faith, hope, and
     encouragement, or are they negative and
     fear-based?

   - Do my words align with God's promises, or
     do they express doubt, worry, or anger?

3. Commit to change.

   - What words do you use consistently that you
     need to reduce or eliminate because they
     influence you or others negatively?

   - How will you hold yourself accountable for
     this change?

   - What words can you replace these negative
     words with?

4. Reflect prayerfully.

   Ask God to reveal any negative words or say-
   ings you use habitually.

*Father God, help me to recognize any negative or
harmful words I speak. Guide me to speak words
of life, hope, and truth and align my speech with
Your promises. In Jesus' name, amen.*

OPEN DOOR 4: YOUR RELATIONSHIPS

The final open door we'll explore is our relationships. These
include relationships with family, friends, coworkers, your
spouse or the person you are dating, and more. Relationships
play a critical role in shaping our lives—they influence how
we think, what we hear and see, and even what we say. As I

Corinthians 15:33 warns us, "Do not be misled: 'Bad company corrupts good character.'" This doesn't mean you should sever ties with everyone who might have a negative influence—these individuals are often family members or coworkers we interact with regularly. However, it's crucial to recognize the impact these relationships have on your spiritual walk.

Take time to evaluate the relationships in your life that most significantly affect your walk with the Lord. Consider whether you need to spend more time nurturing relationships with those who strengthen your faith or perhaps seek out new, godly friends and mentors. Hebrews 10:24–25 says, "And let us consider one another in order to stir up love and good works, not forsaking the assembling of ourselves together, as is the manner of some, but exhorting one another, and so much the more as you see the Day approaching" (NKJV).

Fellowship with other believers is essential for keeping our faith strong. That's why it's so important to connect with a Bible-believing church or a small group of strong Christians who can encourage and disciple you. Isolation weakens our defenses, making us vulnerable to the devil's tactics. The enemy thrives when he can isolate believers because without encouragement and accountability it is much harder to stay strong in faith. Surrounding yourself with like-minded Christians helps you grow spiritually, stay rooted in the truth, and stand firm against challenges.

When I first began sharing my faith online, I struggled with a sense of isolation. Though God was blessing the work, I realized after about a year that I didn't know anyone personally who was doing the same thing. Without a support network, it became difficult to share my struggles and receive encouragement. I prayed, asking God to bring people into my life who understood the unique challenges of online ministry.

God not only answered that prayer, but He exceeded my expectations. Over the next few months He introduced me to incredible individuals, mature in their walks with God, who encouraged me, offered wisdom, and reminded me that I didn't have to walk this path alone. Among them were mentors with decades of experience in ministry whose insights helped me navigate challenges with a perspective I couldn't have gained on my own. This experience highlighted the value of kingdom relationships and the importance of surrounding yourself with people who can sharpen your faith.

I believe there are three types of relationships that are essential to our growth and service in the kingdom. Each one supports, strengthens, and guides us in our walk with God in unique ways.

1. **Relationships with unbelievers or those young in their faith walk.** These relationships, whether with friends, colleagues, or even family members, can be challenging. People who do not share your faith, or are not strong in it, may not understand your values or beliefs. However, these relationships are also crucial because they offer unique opportunities to be a light for Christ. Matthew 5:16 says, "Let your light shine before others."

   These connections allow you to demonstrate God's love, grace, and patience in real and impactful ways. Your presence in their lives might be the only reflection of Christ they see, which can plant seeds of faith and offer hope where it's needed most. By keeping these relationships grounded in prayer, you can maintain healthy boundaries while being a source of encouragement and pointing them toward a life of faith.

2. **Relationships with people at your level of spiritual maturity.** These are often your closest friends—those who are at a similar stage in life and faith. Proverbs 27:17 says, "As iron sharpens iron, so one person sharpens another." These relationships are vital for fellowship, accountability, and mutual encouragement. They allow you to walk alongside people who understand the struggles and triumphs of your faith journey. Fellowship with like-minded believers helps keep you spiritually fueled, offers a place to share burdens and celebrate victories, and bolsters your commitment to living a life that honors God.

3. **Relationships with those ahead of you spiritually.** Mentors, spiritual leaders, and others who are more mature in their faith offer invaluable guidance. Hebrews 13:7 reminds us to "consider the outcome of their way of life and imitate their faith." Being mentored by someone with a deeper understanding of God's Word can help you discern God's will, avoid pitfalls, and develop spiritual discipline. They can also offer accountability, wisdom, and encouragement rooted in experience and maturity. These relationships remind us that growth is a journey, and learning from those who have

walked it longer than we have helps us reach
new depths in our relationship with God.

Closing the door

Use this exercise to take a closer look at your relationships, evaluating how each one influences your spiritual growth and kingdom goals.

1. List the people you spend the most time with, including family, friends, coworkers, and mentors.

2. Reflect on the influence of each relationship; for each person consider:

   • Do they encourage my faith and values, or do they lead me toward negative behaviors or compromise?

   • Do I feel spiritually filled or uplifted after spending time with them, or do I feel drained or distracted?

3. Commit to change.

   • Whom do you need to spend more or less time with to improve your life spiritually, mentally, and emotionally?

   • What types of relationships are missing in your life?

   • How will you hold yourself accountable for this change?

4. Reflect prayerfully.

   Ask God for wisdom in evaluating your

relationships and to bring new, strong believers into your life.

Heavenly Father, reveal any relationships that may be drawing me away from You. Give me the courage to set boundaries with those who don't align with Your purpose for my life. Help me connect with strong believers who will build me up in faith and keep me accountable to stay on fire for You. In Jesus' name, amen.

KEEPING THE DOORS CLOSED

Even years after I was healed from mental illness and the demonic oppression I endured, the enemy would still occasionally try to return with his lies. A couple of times a year a thought would creep into my mind, asking, "What if it comes back?" The enemy was trying to plant seeds of doubt. The difference is that I understood my identity in Christ and how to resist those lies by speaking God's truth over my life each time a doubt arose.

So, too, when you discover an open door in your life and use God's Word and your authority as a believer to close it, you must continue to walk in His truth daily. Ephesians 6:10–11 says, "Finally, be strong in the Lord and in his mighty power. Put on the full armor of God, so that you can take your stand against the devil's schemes."

Staying rooted in God's truth will keep those doors closed, and we do that by putting on the armor of God.

STAYING PROTECTED WITH THE ARMOR OF GOD

We live in two realms—the physical world, which we can see and experience, and the spiritual world, which we cannot see but can sometimes sense. As children of God we are called to walk by faith and not by sight. Our faith in God's Word must take precedence over what our physical senses tell us, especially in matters of healing and well-being.

In the unseen spiritual realm there is constant warfare. Though we may not perceive it with our eyes, the Holy Spirit often allows us to sense its reality. Ephesians 6:10 reminds us to "be strong in the Lord and in the power of His might" (NKJV) because our struggles are not against flesh and blood but against spiritual forces of evil, including principalities, powers, rulers of the darkness, and spiritual wickedness in high places.

The apostle Paul uses the metaphor of a fully armored Roman soldier to illustrate how a Christian should be equipped and ready for spiritual battle.

> Therefore, put on every piece of God's armor so you will be able to resist the enemy in the time of evil. Then after the battle you will still be standing firm. Stand your ground, putting on the belt of truth and the body armor of God's righteousness. For shoes, put on the peace that comes from the Good News so that you will be fully prepared. In addition to all of these, hold up the shield of faith to stop the fiery arrows of the devil. Put on salvation as your helmet, and take the sword of the Spirit, which is the word of God. Pray in the Spirit at all times and on every

occasion. Stay alert and be persistent in your prayers
for all believers everywhere.

—EPHESIANS 6:13–18, NLT

Imagine a soldier, fully clad in armor, standing firm with a
shield and sword in hand. Similarly, we are instructed to put
on the whole armor of God to stand strong against the enemy's schemes. The enemy operates through lies and deception,
seeking to steal, kill, and destroy. But God has provided us
with five defensive pieces of armor and one powerful offensive
weapon, the Word of God, which even Jesus used when Satan
tempted Him in the wilderness.

- **The belt of truth**—This protected the soldier's
  loins and held all the armor in place, including
  the sword. Similarly, for us as Christians, truth
  holds everything else together. To resist the
  enemy's lies, we must know the truth, which is
  rooted in understanding God's Word and our
  identity and authority in Christ.

- **The breastplate of righteousness**—Just as
  the ancient breastplate protected the soldier's
  vital organs, so the breastplate of righteousness guards our most spiritually vital organ:
  the heart. This breastplate is held in place by
  the belt of truth, symbolizing how righteousness is grounded in truth. As Christians we
  are clothed in the righteousness of Christ,
  who exchanged our sins for His righteousness on the cross. When God sees us, He sees
  the righteousness of Christ. We are righteous
  not because of anything we did but because of

Jesus' finished work on the cross. Knowing this protects us from the accusations and attacks of the enemy.

- **The shoes of peace**—A Roman soldier's shoes had hobnails on the sides, sort of like football cleats, which kept his footing secure in battle. As a Christian you are to have "strapped on your feet the gospel of peace in preparation [to face the enemy with firm-footed stability and the readiness produced by the good news]" (Eph. 6:15, AMP).

  We must always be ready to share the good news that God loved us so much that He sent Jesus to redeem us. And we must be prepared to stand our ground when the enemy attacks. For instance, when Satan reminds us of our past, we can dig our shoes of peace into God's Word and declare that we are new creations in Christ; the old has passed away, and all things have become new (2 Cor. 5:17). Again, when we know who we are and the authority we have in Christ, we will be ready to stand firm in the truth no matter what the enemy brings (2 Thess. 2:15).

- **The shield of faith**—The Roman soldier used his shield to protect himself from the enemy's arrows, spears, and swords. The shield of faith is the armor that extinguishes the fiery arrows of the enemy, namely doubts, unbelief, and lies. As our faith grows through God's Word, these attacks cannot penetrate our hearts. Satan can cast all of his weapons against us, but they will not be able to harm us.

- **The helmet of salvation**—The soldier's helmet protected his head, and the helmet of salvation similarly guards our minds. Through Christ we are assured of salvation and forgiven of sin. His Spirit confirms we are children of God and guides us into all truth (John 16:13). We must protect our thoughts by renewing our minds daily with God's Word and trust that He has given us a sound mind (2 Tim. 1:7, NKJV).

- **The sword of the Spirit**, which is the Word of God—This is our only offensive weapon. Jesus wielded it against Satan during His temptations in the wilderness, countering each attack with Scripture. In the face of fear, doubt, sickness, or any challenge, we too must use God's Word to fight back. His Word is powerful, sharper than any weapon in Satan's arsenal and more than able to drive away the devil and his forces of darkness.

To stand firm in spiritual battles, we must be fully armed from head to toe and persistent in prayer. When seeking healing, especially for mental health conditions, we must root ourselves in the truth of God's provision for healing. Strongholds of doubt and unbelief must be torn down. By standing on God's Word and His promises, empowered by His Spirit, we can overcome the enemy and remain steadfast in faith.

Chapter 14

HOW TO PRAY FOR THOSE WITH MENTAL HEALTH CHALLENGES

A s I LOOK back on the mental health crisis I faced, one thing that stands out is the invaluable support of strong believers who were praying for me. The prayers of my mom, family, Christian friends, and pastor became a lifeline for me during times when I struggled to pray for myself. Even though they couldn't fully understand what I was going through, their faith in God and His ability to meet my need never wavered. I vividly remember times when I was gripped by paranoia and delusion and they would lay hands on me and pray powerfully, even when I responded with confusion and dismay. Their boldness, faith, and willingness to show up for me ultimately helped me believe I could make it through—and that I too could pray and trust God for healing.

If you have loved ones facing difficult mental health challenges like I did, I encourage you to become a prayer warrior. Stand in faith and pray for them, trusting that your prayers can bring comfort, strength, and healing in their time of need. In 1 Timothy 2:1, Paul urges us to "to pray for all people. Ask God to help them; intercede on their behalf, and give thanks for them" (NLT). No matter where you are in your prayer journey, the Holy Spirit can guide you in praying for your loved one through their mental health struggles. To intercede means to intervene on someone else's behalf. You don't need a theology degree or special status in the church to do that. James 5:16 reminds us that "the prayer of a righteous person is powerful and effective." You have everything you need right now to start interceding for others.

Let's explore some key considerations for praying for those dealing with mental health challenges, including specific prayers you can use to address their needs.

RECOGNIZE THE LAYERS OF MENTAL HEALTH STRUGGLES

When praying for someone facing mental health challenges, it's important to remember that these struggles often stem from a variety of factors. These may include biological influences like genetics or brain chemistry, psychological elements such as past trauma or negative thought patterns, environmental stressors like financial hardship or relationship struggles, and spiritual battles where discouragement or lies from the enemy may play a role. Recognizing these layers helps us pray with compassion and understanding as the Holy Spirit leads.

Depending on the severity of the person's situation and their openness to prayer, you may choose to pray with them in person or intercede from a distance. Don't let someone's lack of openness to prayer discourage you from interceding for them. Whether you pray in person or from afar, your prayers make a difference. Always approach the situation with compassion and humility. Colossians 3:12 reminds us, "As God's chosen people, holy and dearly loved, clothe yourselves with compassion, kindness, humility, gentleness, and patience." Prayer may not instantly fix their situation, but it's a powerful way to invite God's presence, comfort, and peace into their lives.

When I pray for anyone going through mental health struggles, I pray from a place of faith, meaning I believe God is who He says He is and that He can and will deliver and heal them. But even if He doesn't in that moment, I continue to pray and believe, as the Bible encourages us to "pray without ceasing" (1 Thess. 5:17, NKJV)—to keep bringing our needs to God and not give up. If you feel discouraged by unanswered prayers, remember God's Word says, "'My grace is all you need. My power works best in weakness.' So now I am glad to boast about my weaknesses, so that the power of Christ can work through me" (2 Cor. 12:9, NLT). This verse is a powerful reminder that God's grace is enough, even when healing doesn't come as we expect. Despite the way things seem, God's power is at work.

PRAYERS WHEN INTERCEDING FROM A DISTANCE

It's important to understand what a person is facing in their mental health journey so we can pray specifically. Be open to asking those you're praying for if there is anything in particular they'd like prayer for. If they aren't comfortable sharing details, you can still pray generally for their mental health, inviting God's healing and peace into their situation.

Here are some prayers for various mental health challenges that may help those for whom you're interceding. Feel free to personalize these prayers with specific names and situations.

Peace

> *Father God, I bring [name] before You and ask You to cover them in peace today. As they deal with [mental health issue], I pray that You remind them that they are fearfully and wonderfully made. Remove this [mental health issue] from their life*

and heal them from the top of their head to the bottom of their feet. In Jesus' name, amen.

Healing and strength

Heavenly Father, I lift up [name] to You, believing that Your miracle-working power is active and moving in their life at this moment. As they face [mental health issue], give them the strength and confidence to know that Your grace is sufficient for them. May You bring full and complete restoration to their body and mind today. In Jesus' name, amen.

Protection

Father God, I pray for [name] and Your complete protection over their mental health. Whatever has been affected, I believe right now that You are restoring and bringing it back to complete and perfect balance. Shield them with the strength to keep walking by faith so they can live in the light of Your glory. In Jesus' name, amen.

Restoration

Heavenly Father, I lift up [name] as they navigate the challenges of [mental health issue]. I pray that You bring healing to every area of their mind and heart that has been affected. Repair their sense of wholeness and bring Your love and comforting presence in every moment of pain. Remind [name] that You will never leave them nor forsake them and that You are bringing them to a full and complete recovery. In Jesus' name, amen.

Healing and freedom

Father God, I lift up [name] to You and ask that [mental health issue] be removed from their life right now in the mighty name of Jesus. Your Word says You forgive all my sins and heal all my diseases (Ps. 103:3), and I stand on that promise today. I believe You are bringing healing and freedom to [name] from every trace of [mental health issue] they are facing. Thank You for Your love and faithfulness. In Jesus' name, amen.

To silence fear and doubt

Heavenly Father, I pray for [name] and the weight of [mental health issue] they're facing. Bring peace to any racing thoughts they may be facing, and silence any and all voices of fear or self-doubt. Fill [name] with wisdom, peace, and a renewed sense of hope in who You are and how much You love them. Help them remember that they are not alone, and give them the courage to trust You during this time. In Jesus' name, amen.

A renewed mind

Father God, I lift up [name] to You and pray for You to renew their mind today. May all the [mental health issue] thoughts be silenced, and may You bring them into a place of peace and security. Anoint and fill them with Your Holy Spirit so they can walk in victory and be free from [mental health issue]. In Jesus' name, amen.

To tear down limiting beliefs and strongholds

Father God, in Jesus' name I lift up [name] to You and ask that You tear down any lies, limiting beliefs, or strongholds the enemy has placed in their life through [mental health issue]. Remove anything standing between [name] and the future You have planned for them. You are their hope and strength, and with You all things are possible. Help [name] to stand firm on the finished work of Jesus, knowing that no weapon formed against them will prosper (Isa. 54:17, NKJV). Thank You, Lord, for Your love, protection, and healing over their life. In Jesus' mighty name, amen.

To close open doors to demonic attack

Heavenly Father, in the name of Jesus I lift up [name] to You and ask that You close any doors in their life that are not in line with Your will. Cancel the enemy's plans over [name] and remove any fear, anxiety, or [mental health issue] that is holding them back. I trust You will completely cover [name] with Your power, love, and peace. Break any chains of addiction, oppression, or struggle with [mental health issue], and let [name] experience the fullness of Your glory and blessings. I claim Your peace and provision over every area of their life. In Jesus' name, amen.

To calm anxious thoughts

Father God, I lift up [name] to You and ask for Your peace to calm their anxious thoughts today as they deal with [mental health issue]. Your Word tells us not to worry but to bring everything to You in prayer, so I ask You now to remove anything troubling their mind. Thank You for filling [name] with joy and for the promise that every plan meant to harm them will fail. In Jesus' name, amen.

Support

Heavenly Father, I pray that You help [name] find the support and resources they need for [mental health issue]. Give [name] the wisdom and guidance to seek counsel from people who uplift them and professionals who can help them in their healing journey. Remind them that You are with them every step of the way, protecting them from all harm and evil. In Jesus' name, amen.

Comfort and joy

Father God, I ask that You guide [name] through [mental health issue], helping them find joy and comfort in every part of their day. Remind them that the joy of the Lord is their strength, and that You are their refuge and help in every time of trouble (Neh. 8:10; Ps. 46:1). Equip [name] to take every negative thought captive in obedience to Christ so they may experience Your peace. In Jesus' name, amen.

Positive, healthy relationships

Heavenly Father, as [name] navigates [mental health issue], I pray that You bring new, supportive, and loving relationships into their life. Surround them with strong believers who can encourage them, pray with them, and remind them of Your goodness. Guard and protect [name] from any relationships that might discourage or hinder their journey toward healing. May Your Word and presence remain strong in their life. In Jesus' name, amen.

Rest

Heavenly Father, bring [name] rest as they continue to work through [mental health issue]. May You grant them restful sleep, physical restoration, and peaceful thoughts throughout their day. Help them also find rest in Your presence as they seek You in this season. Give them the wisdom to navigate [mental health issue] in a way that honors You and brings healing. Thank You for being their constant source of comfort and peace. In Jesus' name, amen.

Endurance

Father God, I ask that You grant [name] the endurance to walk by faith each day, believing in Your promise of permanent healing from [mental health issue]. Help [name] find purpose in this season and hold on to hope, no matter what their current situation may look like. Remind them that You work all things together for good and that You are not done working on them, in them, and through them. In Jesus' name, amen.

SPECIFIC AREAS TO COVER IN PRAYER

When interceding for someone facing a mental health challenge, take a moment to consider specific areas of need you can cover in prayer. These might include prayers for the following:

- **Patience and grace**—Many people struggle with patience and giving themselves grace when their situation doesn't seem to be changing. Pray for God to pour out His grace and patience upon them during this season.

- **Healthy relationships**—The enemy loves to target isolated believers, and the pull to withdraw can be even stronger when a person is battling mental health struggles. Pray for God to bring new, healthy relationships into the person's life to encourage them and strengthen their faith. Pray also for God to remove anyone who may be hindering the person's faith or negatively influencing their thoughts, even if you don't know who those people might be.

- **Physical wellness and rest**—We can't ignore the importance of rest and caring for our bodies, as these directly impact our mental health. For someone facing high levels of anxiety, prioritizing rest and physical well-being can be a key step toward healing.

- **Freedom from shame**—For those experiencing severe mental health challenges, the weight of stigmas and shame can be heavy. Pray for the person to find confidence in who they are in Christ and to stand firm in His love.

- **Purpose and meaning**—It's common for those suffering from mental health struggles to believe the lie that their lives lack meaning. Pray that God would help them see the purpose they were created for and the unique calling on their life.

- **Decision-making**—Mental health challenges can impair decision-making, leading to further heartache. Pray that God grants the person wisdom to make choices that are good for them, bless others, and please Him.

- **Loneliness**—Proverbs 13:12 says "hope deferred makes the heart sick." Loneliness can deepen heartache and make people feel forgotten or unseen. Pray that God would bring comfort to those who are lonely and remind them that they are seen and loved.

- **Isolation and withdrawal**—During mental health struggles, it's easy to withdraw from relationships and responsibilities. Pray that God gives the person the courage and strength to stay connected with loved ones and those who can support them in this critical time.

- **Hope for the future**—For those facing ongoing mental health challenges, hope can feel out of reach. Yet faith is "the substance of things hoped for, the evidence of things not seen" (Heb. 11:1, NKJV). Pray that your loved one holds on to hope and trusts that God has a good future for them as promised in Jeremiah 29:11.

- **Willingness to seek help**—Sometimes those we care about may resist seeking help for their mental health struggles. Pray for them to have the humility and openness to seek both spiritual and professional support, and ask God to place other believers in their lives whose encouragement they may be more willing to receive.

As you can see, many aspects of a person's life can impact their mental health. While it's important to pray specifically for their mental health struggle, remember to also pray over these other areas, as any one of them may be significantly affecting their life. This approach strengthens our prayer life too, helping us stay consistent in lifting our loved ones up to God and follow Paul's wisdom to "never stop praying" (1 Thess. 5:17, NLT).

CONSIDERATIONS WHEN PRAYING IN PERSON

Sometimes you may only have the opportunity to pray for someone from a distance, but if they're open to praying in person with you, I encourage you to take that step. Jesus tells us that where two or three are gathered in His name, He is there in the midst of them (Matt. 18:20). Praying with someone you love is powerful, though it may feel intimidating. You might worry about finding the right words or wonder how the other person will respond—but take heart! The Holy Spirit is with you, ready to help.

Romans 8:26–27 reminds us that "the Holy Spirit helps us in our weakness. For example, we don't know what God wants us to pray for. But the Holy Spirit prays for us with groanings that cannot be expressed in words. And the Father who knows all hearts knows what the Spirit is saying, for the Spirit pleads for us believers in harmony with God's own will" (NLT). Invite the Holy Spirit to minister to you as you pray for your loved one.

Here are a few considerations when praying with someone in person.

Ask for permission and respect their comfort level.

Before praying, ask if they're comfortable with you praying for them in that moment. If you usually place a hand on someone's shoulder or hold their hand while praying, ask if they're OK with that as well.

Focus on faith, hope, and encouragement, not "fixing" them.

When praying for someone struggling with a mental health challenge, be mindful not to pray in a way that implies something is "wrong" with them. Focus on God's Word, standing in faith on His promises for hope, healing, and restoration.

Offer your continued support.

Don't let prayer be your only form of support. Remind them that you're available if they need someone to talk to, and offer any practical support you can provide. Sometimes just knowing someone genuinely cares can make a big difference.

God has called you to be a prayer warrior—not because you have years of experience or special qualifications, but because you've chosen to step into this meaningful role by supporting someone with prayer. You may be the only one praying for that loved one fighting for their mental health. You may think what you're doing is small, but you are a lifeline as you stand in faith on their behalf and bring their needs before God. Take this role seriously, knowing that your prayers are powerful and effective (Jas. 5:16).

You don't have to be perfect for your prayers to bear fruit; you just need a willing heart. As you grow as a prayer warrior, you'll find that God strengthens and equips you as you seek Him. Trust that He hears every word and that through your prayers you are helping to lay a foundation of faith, hope, healing, and support for those you love.

Step up and become the prayer warrior your friends and family need. Let your commitment to prayer be a source of strength, peace, and faith—not only for you but also for those God has placed on your heart. Remember, God is with you in every prayer you offer, and each one matters.

Chapter 15

DAILY PRAYERS FOR HEALING, STRENGTH, AND PEACE

WE'VE EXPLORED THE vital connection between mental health and the power of prayer in your daily life. My hope is that this has given you a strong foundation to face any mental health challenges with confidence—rooted in prayer, your knowledge of who you are in Christ, and the authority given to you as a believer.

If you haven't already, take some time to revisit the exercises shared. These are designed to help you identify and break free from any lies, open doors, or strongholds through prayer and a deeper relationship with the Lord.

Your mental health is important, and renewing your mind through God's Word and presence is key. This requires obedience, discipline, and a steadfast commitment to keeping God as the priority in your life. Remember, your personal prayer time with the Lord equips you to walk in victory each day and to cover your loved ones in prayer.

As we conclude this book, I want to share a collection of daily personal prayers for healing, strength, and peace. Despite having experienced God's supernatural healing in my life, I still pray each day for ongoing healing over my mind and body. This helps me stand on God's promises and keeps the enemy from gaining any footholds in my life.

If you're still waiting on God for healing, don't let the enemy quench your flame. Use these prayers to stay strong in your faith and trust God for healing, and return to them as often as you need to in order to keep your prayer life growing and strong.

PRAYERS FOR PEACE AND PROTECTION

Father God, I am so thankful that You have given me a place of safety when I put my trust in You. You give me peace and contentment in my mind, and You protect me from physical and spiritual harm. I command all evil spirits and forces of darkness that seek to harm me to depart from me now. In Jesus' name, amen.

Father God, thank You for being my refuge and strength, an ever-present help in trouble (Ps. 46:1). In You, I find peace and security, knowing You guard my mind, heart, and body. Continue to lead me on the right path so I can accomplish all that You have called me to do. I trust You and thank You for Your goodness and presence in my life. In Jesus' name, amen.

Heavenly Father, I am grateful that You surround me with Your protection. Thank You for filling my mind with peace and my heart with confidence. I choose to walk joyfully with You, knowing that Your peace and protection remove all fear, worry, and anxiety in my life. In Jesus' name, amen.

Heavenly Father, thank You for being my rock and foundation when I feel insecure or unsteady. I find strength and confidence in You, knowing that no matter what challenges I face, You are with me, guiding and helping me in every area of my life. I trust that today will be a great day, filled with Your presence. In Jesus' name, amen.

Father God, thank You for caring about every detail of my life. In a world that feels chaotic and unsettling, I'm grateful for the peace You give—a peace that calms me, strengthens me, and fills me with courage. I declare that fear has no place in my life, and I receive Your peace. In Jesus' name, amen.

Father God, today is a new day, and I am grateful that I can bring my concerns, anxieties, and worries about [share specifics with God] to You. I ask You to move in these areas where I feel weak [make your requests], and I thank You for hearing me and answering me. I receive Your peace concerning these issues, and I rest in Your presence. In Jesus' name, amen.

Heavenly Father, sometimes I feel overwhelmed by anxiety and stress and I just need Your peace to calm me down. Help me remember to bring all my concerns to You, even the minor ones, and trust You to handle them. Today I give You [tell the Lord what they are], and I receive Your peace in exchange. I know worry changes nothing, but You have the power to transform every situation. Thank You for Your love and care for me and my family. In Jesus' name, amen.

Father God, thank You for giving me peace of mind when I feel stressed, face problems, and feel lost. You said that life would have its troubles, but I don't need to be stressed because You have overcome the world (John 16:33). Help me to find joy even in the midst of life's challenges. In Jesus' name, amen.

Heavenly Father, I thank You that I am Your child. When I feel rejected or unloved by friends or family, I am reassured that Your love for me never fails or changes. You promised never to abandon me, even when I stray because of my unwise choices or difficult circumstances. You have said You would bless me with peace, so I receive Your strength and the blessing of Your peace right now. In Jesus' name, amen.

Father God, I thank You that You are my peace. Whenever I feel insecure, I know I can call on You for help and comfort. Your Holy Spirit is always with me, and the peace that comes from You is beyond my understanding. I may not fully grasp it, but I know I have peace because I have You, and You will never leave me nor forsake me. In Jesus' name, amen.

Heavenly Father, I am so grateful for the secret place of safety You've provided, where You protect and shield me from the dangers and attacks of the enemy. You fill my mind with peace and contentment and guard me from both physical and spiritual harm. Help me to trust in You fully, especially when I feel anxiety pressing in. I command every evil spirit and demonic force that seeks to harm me to depart now, in Jesus' name. Amen.

I thank You, Father, that Your presence fills my heart and soul with joy and peace. Because of Your promises, I can live with confidence and hope, knowing that Your Word is truth. Help me to stay in faith without wavering and to focus on Your promises rather than my current circumstances. I trust that Your Word has the power to change my reality from darkness to light. In Jesus' name, amen.

PRAYERS FOR STRENGTH AND CONFIDENCE

Father God, You are so wonderful and powerful. When I need hope in times of stress and worry, You remind me that the joy of the Lord is my strength (Neh. 8:10). No matter the negative circumstances I face right now, fill me with Your joy and strength so I can remember that You will always bring me through and make me strong. In Jesus' name, amen.

Heavenly Father, I thank You that Your Word is strong and powerful and is my guide to successful living. I trust Your Word and receive Your Spirit, which empowers me to love myself and others, overcome fear, and have a sound mind. I am self-disciplined, and I exercise good judgment with Your love and confident hope in my heart. Grant me courage and boldness this day. In Jesus' name, amen.

Father God, thank You for this new day You have blessed me with. I can be confident, courageous, and brave because You are always with me. Even in my weakness You strengthen and uphold me. Your Word tells me not to fear, but at times life's circumstances cause my body to react with anxiety and stress. I declare victory over those moments, for You, O Lord, are my strength and firm foundation. In Jesus' name, amen.

Thank You, Father God, for Your unfailing love and for bringing me into this world with the gift of life. You loved me so much that You sent Your Son, Jesus, to pay for my sins and shortcomings. Through Him, I have been reborn into Your family, and now I am Your child with the promise of eternal life in heaven and abundant life here on earth. Your perfect love casts out all fear, which often tries to torment my mind and heart (1 John 4:8). Your love within me continues to grow, driving out every fear that comes to defeat me. Help me to be strong and courageous in sharing Your love and goodness with others. In Jesus' name, amen.

Thank You, Lord, that I am blessed each day—not because I deserve it or have earned it but simply because I am Your child and You love me. I walk in Your favor because You go before me, You are with me, and You will never leave me or give up on me. I trust that even when I mess up repeatedly, You are always there to help me. Others may abandon me or treat me poorly, but I can always depend on You because Your love for me is unwavering. In Jesus' name, amen.

Father God, You are so good and approachable. I thank You that I can come to You with confidence, knowing You care about every detail of my life. Even the small things that might bother me, You are there to help with. I trust that Your will for me includes salvation, a growing and intimate relationship with You, physical and spiritual healing, and the blessing of an abundant life. Help me to believe Your Word with unshakable confidence and to trust Your promises without doubt or unbelief. In Jesus' name, amen.

Thank You, Jesus, for empowering me with the strength to accomplish what I couldn't do on my own. You've placed dreams in my heart, and as I take steps of faith, You open doors of opportunity and grant me favor with those I encounter. I step out with confidence in You, trusting that what You have birthed in my heart will come to pass by Your grace and power. I dare to dream big, take action, and proclaim Your goodness. In Jesus' name, amen.

Heavenly Father, thank You for being an awesome and powerful God. I reach out to You with hope and joy, knowing that Your strength is available when I'm stressed or worried. I don't have to rely on my own strength, for when I am weak, You remind me to say, "I am strong." Thank You for empowering me to endure and overcome life's challenges. In Jesus' name, amen.

Father God, thank You for making me strong, healthy, wealthy, and wise, capable of doing all things through You and Your anointing. Grant me the wisdom and strength to live the abundant life Jesus paid the price to give me—a life filled with love, joy, and fulfillment. Help me to grow closer to You each day and to become more like You in every way. In Jesus' name, amen.

Father God, I am so grateful that You are always with me. Life isn't always easy, and sometimes I feel burdened by my thoughts, actions, or what others may think of me. I call on You in these struggles, trusting You to rescue me from any mess I may or may not have caused. I trust that You know me intimately, You love me unconditionally, and You take care of me because I am Yours. In Jesus' name, amen.

Thank You, Father God, that I don't have to rely solely on myself to make wise choices and decisions. Your Word reminds me to trust in You and acknowledge You in all that I do, and You will guide my steps (Prov. 3:5–6). I depend on Your Holy Spirit to lead me and make my path smooth. When I face big decisions and feel uncertain, I trust that You will speak to my heart, giving me insight and confidence. And if I later find I've made a mistake, I have full assurance that You will lovingly correct my course. In Jesus' name, amen.

Thank You, Father God, for being so merciful and gracious and for loving me because I am Your child. I know that Jesus paid for all my sins—past, present, and future—and even though I may mess up, make wrong choices, and fail to please You, I can always come boldly to You and ask for Your forgiveness and help without any fear that You will turn me away. Your amazing grace and love are always there to help me change and become a better person. Because You first loved me, I love You. In Jesus' name, amen.

Father God, I am so thankful that I am in Your thoughts and You have great plans for me and my future, plans to prosper me and give me confident hope and strength (Jer. 29:11). Help me to recognize my gifts and calling, and give me the courage to pursue my dreams. Open the right doors, and close those that are not in Your plans for my life. In Jesus' name, amen.

Heavenly Father, I am so thankful that I can rely on You and Your tender mercies, which are new every morning. When I feel down about things I've said, negative thoughts, weaknesses, or failures, You surround me with Your loving-kindness and lift me up to find victory. In Jesus' name, amen.

I thank You, Father, that Your favor and grace empower me to live a victorious life. In my weaknesses and shortcomings, You display Your power, strengthening me daily. You are all I need to accomplish everything You've called me to do, and I am thankful. In Jesus' name, amen.

PRAYERS FOR HEALING AND DELIVERANCE

Thank You, Lord, that I can call on You for help, especially when I feel trapped in a behavior, habit, mindset, or difficult circumstance. You are my rescuer and protector, even when sickness or disease comes against me. I command all illness and disease to leave my body and mind now. In Jesus' name, amen.

Lord, I thank You that in times of trouble, I can rely on You to keep me safe from all evil forces, viruses, and diseases. You are my God and my protector; my faith and trust are in You. In Jesus' name I declare that no evil, plague, virus, or disease will come near me, my family, or my home. Any virus that tries to attach itself to me will die in Jesus' mighty name. I am strong, healthy, wealthy, and wise because of Your faithfulness. In Jesus' name, amen.

Father God, I thank You that I can be secure knowing that any physical or spiritual attack or weapon that comes against me will not succeed. I am an overcomer because You are my strength in challenging times. Help me to trust in Your love for me when an attack from the enemy comes my way. In Jesus' name, amen.

Father God, I thank You that I can find security in knowing that no physical or spiritual attack or weapon formed against me will succeed. You are my strength in challenging times, and because of

You, I am an overcomer. Help me to trust in Your unwavering love when the enemy targets my body, mind, or spirit. Remind me of Your protection and fill me with peace and resilience. In Jesus' name, amen.

Thank You, Lord, that by Your stripes I am healed (Isa. 53:5, NKJV). Each stripe You endured was for the healing of every disease, injury, and broken place in my body and mind. Right now I speak healing over myself, from the top of my head to the soles of my feet. I receive complete healing—physical, mental, emotional, and spiritual—in Your mighty name, Jesus. Amen.

Lord God, Your Word says that life and death are in the power of the tongue (Prov. 18:21). Remind me to be mindful of my words, knowing they have power and activate spiritual forces, either for me or against me. I cancel any negative words or curses spoken over me, including those I may have spoken myself. Instead, I declare the life-giving truth from Your Word—that I am strong, healthy, and walk daily in divine health. In Jesus' name, amen.

Thank You, Lord, that my faith grows each day. Your Word says that faith comes by hearing the Word of God (Rom. 10:17), and as I listen to Your promises concerning healing, my faith is strengthened. I declare and receive healing in my body [name the specific ailment or injury], and I thank You that Your healing power is at work in me right now. I may not see it instantly, but I continue to

*believe and receive what I have asked for. In Jesus'
name, amen.*

*I thank You, Father God, that You desire to give
me good things, including strength and health in
my body and mind. Your love for me is beyond
anything I can imagine—You even know the
number of hairs on my head. I know You are a
loving Father who gives good gifts to His children,
and I ask for and receive Your healing and health
in my mind and body. In Jesus' name I command
sickness, disease, and weakness to leave my body
now. Amen.*

*Lord, I thank You that I can come to You just as I
am. I don't have to earn Your love or pay any price
because Jesus paid it all when He took my punishment on the cross. I ask that You strengthen and
heal my body [name the specific issue] quickly. I
command all unbelief and doubt to leave my mind
right now. In Jesus' name, amen.*

*Lord, I know that healing is a gift for Your chil-
dren, and I am Your child. My mind and mental
state need healing. At times, I experience unsettling thoughts and feel as though I'm losing control.
I plead the blood of Jesus over my head, my brain,
and my mind. Any unclean or oppressive spirit
trying to bring me down I command to leave me
now, in Jesus' mighty name. Holy Spirit, I ask You
to fill me, protecting me from any demonic forces
that come against me. In Jesus' name, amen.*

Lord Jesus, You came to save, heal, and set me free. I need Your power to break the chains of addiction [name the specific addiction] that are controlling me. I want to take back control over my life and be free from the urges, substances, habits, and indulgences that currently rule over me. Right now, I declare the power of addiction broken over my life. Thank You, Lord, for helping me each day, making it easier to walk in freedom and self-control. In Jesus' name, amen.

Thank You, Lord, that You care deeply about my feelings and are with me in times of emotional pain and suffering. You said You came to heal the brokenhearted and wounded, so I ask You to mend my heart and make it whole. Fill me with Your peace, love, and joy so I may live an abundant life. In Jesus' name, amen.

Father God, I pray for the health and well-being of myself, my family, and my friends. Bless and protect us from all harm and evil, and remove anything that may bring sickness or suffering. By Your stripes we are healed, and I thank You, Lord, for always watching over us. Help us to trust in Your healing power and to walk in the fullness of health You have promised. In Jesus' name, amen.

Father God, I'm going through some battles right now—some physical and others mental—and I trust that You are my source of healing, restoration, and redemption. I receive my healing right now in the mighty and matchless name of Jesus. Amen.

Father, thank You for this wonderful day that You have given me. I look forward to a blessed and productive day. Help me to keep my thoughts focused on who You say I am—blessed, favored, healed, prosperous, deeply loved, above and not beneath, the head and not the tail. In Jesus' name, amen.

Father God, thank You for comforting me, even in the midst of my mental health struggles. Your Word reminds me that my identity is not defined by my crisis but by who I am in Christ. Today I speak healing over my mind and thank You for renewing it daily. Grant me the courage to stand firm and fight against any attacks of the enemy. In Jesus' name, amen.

Heavenly Father, I ask for Your peace to calm my anxious thoughts today. Your Word tells me not to worry but to bring everything to You in prayer (Phil. 4:6), so I ask You now to remove anything that troubles my mind. Thank You for filling me with joy and for the promise that no weapon formed against me will succeed (Isa. 54:17). In Jesus' name, amen.

Father God, thank You for caring about every detail of my life, both major and minor. You promise that when I come to You with confidence, asking according to Your will, You hear me (1 John 5:14). I know Your will includes my salvation, healing, and the blessings of an abundant life. Help me to believe without doubt or unbelief when I ask You for [your request], because with You all things are possible (Matt. 19:26). I am a strong believer, and I see You working in my life. In Jesus' name, amen.

Heavenly Father, I speak against any oppression I'm facing and rebuke it in the name of Jesus. Your Word says the truth will make me free, and in Jesus, I am truly free (John 8:32, 36). Thank You for equipping me with everything I need to overcome the enemy's schemes. I claim my total and complete freedom right now, in Jesus' name. Amen.

Father God, I speak against any spiritual warfare affecting my life right now and command it to leave in the name of Jesus. Fear, depart from me now in the name of Jesus. Depression, leave me now in the name of Jesus. Any trauma, be gone now in the name of Jesus. And demonic oppression, leave me now in the name of Jesus. I declare that I am free by the blood of Jesus and the word of my testimony (Rev. 12:11). In Jesus' name, amen.

Father God, thank You for protecting my mind and body from sickness and disease. Restore anything in my body that is out of balance, and remove any harmful or repetitive thoughts that seek to keep me trapped. I thank You for complete health and the strength to steward the gifts and calling on my life in a way that pleases You and builds Your kingdom. In Jesus' name, amen.

FAITH FOR THE JOURNEY AHEAD

As we come to the end of this journey together, my hope is that you feel equipped, empowered, and encouraged to face life's challenges with renewed faith and hope. Throughout these pages we've explored the profound connection between prayer and mental health—how prayer can strengthen, restore, and give us the courage to rise above the physical and spiritual battles we face.

Life isn't easy, and struggles with mental health are very real. But you don't face these battles alone. God, in His everlasting love, is with you every step of the way. He cares about every part of you—spirit, soul, and body. He created you with a purpose, and His desire is for you to experience peace, wholeness, and abundant life in Him.

When you're carrying heavy burdens, the enemy may try to sow doubt, fear, and discouragement. But you have authority in Christ, and through prayer you can break the chains that try to hold you back. Every prayer, whether offered in a moment of strength or weakness, is powerful because it connects you to a God who listens, cares, and responds. His Word is your foundation, His Spirit is your comforter, and His promises are your guide.

As you move forward in faith, I encourage you to hold fast to the truths in God's Word. When you feel overwhelmed, remember that God invites you to cast every burden on Him, trusting that He cares for you deeply. Make prayer not just an occasional refuge but a daily rhythm—a source of strength and connection. And don't forget the power of community. Surround yourself with others who will stand by you, pray with you, and remind you of your identity in Christ.

No matter what you face, know that God's love is sufficient.

You are deeply loved, highly favored, and completely accepted by your heavenly Father. He sees every tear, knows every struggle, and walks with you through every trial. Lean into His presence, trust His guidance, and let His peace rule your heart and mind. With God you are capable of enduring, healing, and thriving.

Keep praying, keep believing, and keep moving forward. The journey of faith isn't about perfection—it's about progress. And as you make progress, you'll find that God's power, peace, and joy are yours, enabling you to live in the fullness He has promised. Be encouraged, stay strong, and remember that God has a great hope and future for you and your family.

Appendix

THE MOST IMPORTANT DECISION

THE MOST IMPORTANT decision you will make in your life is to accept Jesus Christ as your personal Lord and Savior. You can't earn your way to heaven or get there simply by living a good life. The only way is through God's Son, Jesus Christ, who came to earth as a man, born of a virgin, and lived a sinless, perfect life. Sin entered the world through one man, Adam, but salvation entered the world through one man, Jesus Christ, the Son of God.

If you have never accepted Jesus as your Savior, consider doing it now with this simple prayer.

PRAYER FOR SALVATION

Heavenly Father, thank You for loving me so much that You sent Your only Son, Jesus, to die on the cross to pay for my sins. I believe that You raised Him from the dead so I could be saved and receive the free gift of eternal life and total salvation.

I am sorry for my sins, and I ask You to change my life and help me live in a way that honors You. Jesus, I ask You to come into my heart, forgive me of all my sins, and be my Lord and Savior. Fill me with Your Holy Spirit, guiding me to live a new life through faith and grace that is pleasing to You. Right now, I declare and confess in faith that I am saved, I am a child of God, and I am a new creation. In the mighty name of Jesus, amen.

If you said that prayer, congratulations, and welcome to the family of God! Making Jesus Christ the Lord of your life is the greatest decision you will ever make. Today, you are a brand-new person in Christ. As the Bible says, "Therefore, if anyone is in Christ, he is a new creation; old things have passed away; behold, all things have become new" (2 Cor. 5:17, NKJV).

Your journey with Christ begins now, and while it will take effort, the rewards are eternal. Start by connecting with a faith-based, Bible-believing church that embraces God's grace and His power for healing and miracles today, a place where you can grow in your faith through discipleship, receive encouragement, and experience the love of God in community.

It may take time to find the right church home, especially if you've experienced hurt in the past. If that's your story, I want to encourage you: Don't give up. Churches are filled with imperfect people, but God's grace is sufficient to heal wounds and lead you to a community that reflects His love. Ask God to guide you to the right place, and trust His timing.

If you have school-age children, look at the children's and youth ministry programs as well. You can go online to hear some of the sermons given by local churches in your area. Select a few churches to visit, and be sure to go more than once before making a decision. If there is a discipleship program, look at that as well.

If you are fighting any type of addiction or need help in your identity in Christ, then consider attending a church that has a Celebrate Recovery program. Sometimes a church can be so big you may feel insignificant. It may be easier to meet new people in a smaller church. Whichever church you choose, consider joining a small group or volunteering so you can make friends with fellow believers.

Also, keep the communication line open to the Lord. Talk with Him like a friend to develop your relationship with Him. As you dive into God's Word each day, let it shape your thoughts, guide your steps, and renew your mind. As Psalm 1:2–3 reminds us, those who meditate on God's Word are like trees planted by streams of water, fruitful and strong, prospering in all they do.

Be sure to sign up for water baptism when it is offered as the next step in your walk with God. Jesus was baptized, and so were the early church members. Water baptism symbolizes our decision to die to the old self and rise up as the new self, or as a new creation in Christ.

Finally, remember this: You are not alone. God is with you every step of the way, and He will complete the good work He has started in you (Phil. 1:6). You have joined a family that spans the globe and eternity.

Welcome to the kingdom of God—your best days are ahead!

Notes

1. Blue Letter Bible, s.v. *"anthistēmi,"* accessed December 9, 2024, https://www.blueletterbible.org/lexicon/g436/ kjv/tr/0-1/.

CHAPTER 7

1. "Mental Health by the Numbers," National Alliance on Mental Illness, accessed December 5, 2024, https:// www.nami.org/about-mental-illness/mental-health- by-the-numbers/.
2. "Mental Health by the Numbers," National Alliance on Mental Illness.
3. Centers for Disease Control, "Mental Health, Substance Use, and Suicidal Ideation During the COVID-19 Pandemic—United States, June 24–30, 2020," *Morbidity and Mortality Weekly Report* 69, no. 32 (August 14, 2020): 1049–57, http://dx.doi. org/10.15585/mmwr.mm6932a1.

CHAPTER 8

1. ONE Research Foundation, "What Changed in the Brain?—Andrew Newberg, MD," April 10, 2019, YouTube video, 2:26, https://www.youtube.com/ watch?v=RiWWPOG3hoA; Andrew Newberg et al., "Cerebral Blood Flow During Meditative Prayer: Preliminary Findings and Methodological Issues," *Perceptual and Motor Skills* 97, no. 2 (October 2003): 625–30, https://doi.org/10.2466/pms.2003.97.2.625; Daniel G. Amen, MD, *The End of Mental Illness* (Tyndale Refresh, 2020), 101–8.
2. Newberg et al., "Cerebral Blood Flow During Meditative Prayer."

CHAPTER 10

1. Prof. Rabbi Rachel Adelman, "Why Did Mordecai Not Bow Down to Haman?," TheTorah.com, accessed December 10, 2024, https://www.thetorah.com/article/why-did-mordecai-not-bow-down-to-haman.

CHAPTER 11

1. Derek Prince, "Protection Against Discouragement and Depression—Part 9 of 15: Where to Find Security," Derek Prince Ministries, accessed December 10, 2024, https://www.derekprince.com/radio/829.

CHAPTER 12

1. Christine Comaford, "Got Inner Peace? 5 Ways to Get It NOW," *Forbes*, November 7, 2013, https://www.forbes.com/sites/christinecomaford/2012/04/04/got-inner-peace-5-ways-to-get-it-now/.

Acknowledgments

THIS BOOK WOULD not have been possible without the grace of God and the unwavering support of my close family and friends who stood by my side, praying and believing in God for my healing. I want to especially thank my wife, Keira; my dad, Don; my brothers, Sean and Ross; and my sister, Danielle. I am also deeply grateful to my grandpa Ralph and his wife, Linda, as well as my cousin Aryan and his family.

Thank you for never giving up on me and for standing in the gap when I couldn't pray or comprehend what was happening during my darkest moments.

I also want to acknowledge everyone who has connected with me through social media over the past five years. Your encouragement, support, and shared faith have given me the unique privilege of putting my story and the lessons God has taught me into this book. Thank you for your overwhelming kindness—partnering with me in prayer, sharing your testimonies, and spreading the power of prayer with those you love. You are a vital part of this journey, and I am deeply grateful for each of you.

About the Author

DAYNE KAMELA IS a social media content creator who shares daily messages on prayer, hope, and encouragement through his platform, @Litwithprayer, with more than 1.4 million followers. His mission is to inspire people to develop a deeper relationship with Jesus through the power of prayer, equipping them to walk in faith, overcome challenges, and live out their God-given purpose.

Kamela also leads the Litwithprayer Foundation, a nonprofit organization that focuses on providing support for young people facing mental health challenges through Christian counseling and on-demand courses, helping them build successful and fulfilling lives. He lives with his wife in Arizona.

A TOOL TO DEEPEN YOUR PRAYER LIFE

Over the past fifteen years, as my prayer life has grown, one common challenge I've faced is that during busy seasons of life, I sometimes found myself praying less often than I would like.

To address this, I established nonnegotiable practices to protect my morning prayer time and other key moments throughout the day. Yet I also wanted to ensure that the distractions of daily life didn't prevent me from staying connected to the Lord.

Knowing that our phones are one of the biggest distractions we carry with us, I set out to create a mobile app that would simply remind me to pray throughout the day—without keeping me even more glued to my screen. From that vision, an app was born.

Unlike other apps, this one was intentionally designed to help you grow in the daily habit of praying more consistently. From providing simple, personal reminders to pray about topics you choose to guided prayers rooted in God's Word that help renew your mind, this app is a tool to keep you spiritually connected and focused on Him.

I invite you to visit prayerprojectapp.com to download the app and try it today. Let's make daily, consistent prayer the foundation of a life centered on God.